Second Chance

Nyengi Koin

Contents

Chapter 1

It was the kind of day that made one feel glad to be alive a glorious day. The sun, shining so bright high up in the sky, sent its light bouncing from roads and white painted walls straight into the eyes of so many of the young people, hurrying about with their bags and suitcases. The bright glass windows sparkled, the brilliant flower-beds blazed white colour. Everyone was in such a pleasant hurry and hardly any of them could see where they were going. Still, no one seemed to mind because they were all in such a good mood.

The College never saw so much hustle and bustle as on days like this — vacation days. There was so much going and coming, in and out of the hostels, and so many people saying goodbye, all in a rush to get home.

The College, the best in Badagry, was well loved by all the students. They were proud of its brilliant academic reputation, proud of the ancient buildings, proud of the large grounds surrounding it, with their various pitches for various games and sports, but most of all, they were proud of the ultra modern new buildings that were the envy of the other higher institutions around. However, despite all these, the students were glad to be going home where they would eat and enjoy some real meals, well cooked and nourishing.

The food was the only bad thing about the College, everyone agreed. The tea could only be described as coloured water, There was hardly ever any tea in it, But all these were part of the joy of living in the College. The students boasted about how bad the food was, just as they boasted about the excellence of everything else.

No one would trade the College for any other. A slim, elegantly dressed girl, with long hair, plaited into a neat bond on the top of her head, was struggling with a mattress under one arm and a suitcase on the other hand. Suddenly she missed a step and nearly fell flat on her face. Then a shadow fell across her line of vision, and she glanced up to see a tall, handsome young man in front of her, arms outstretched to catch her.

'Can I help you with that?' he asked her laughing, pointing to the suitcase.

'Oh please!' she simply replied.

He took the suitcase from her and found that it was quite heavy. Funny how she thought she could manage both this and the mattress, he smiled to himself, with such elegant high heels and a straight skirt too. It wasn't the right type of clothes for weight-lifting at all. He was still smiling as they walked out through the gates, silently considering each other. Outside the hostel security gate, the girl pointed to a grey Leyland Range Rover. A chau-ffeur, clad in blue lined French suit, came hurrying to take the mattress from her. He opened the door and both the suitcase and the mattress were thrown on the back seat. Then they both walked back into the hostel yard together.

I was watching you from the door of the conference room. Why are you taking the mattress home?' he asked her, curiosity getting the better of him. "It's mine. I didn't fancy the one on my bed here, it was so hard, you see, so I brought that one from home.'

"So you take it back at the end of term?' he asked again, amusement written all over his face.

'Of course not,' She said, smiling too. "That would look funny. It's my last day here. I've just finished my course so I'm taking all my things home,' she explained happily.

'How lucky can you get? Well, congratulations! I've still got another year to go. What did you study?' I've just finished my course in Business Studies.'

'Ah, what a nice course. I'm taking a degree course in Management Studies.' He hesitated in front of Helena Hall, one of the girls' hostels. 'Do you still have any luggage you'd like me to help you with?'

'Yes, if you don't mind, please. I've got one more suitcase and a lot of other little things to take home,' she said hesitantly.

She had so much luggage and so many little bits and pieces that he wondered what she needed all of them for while still a student. She hadn't lacked a single thing, as far as he could see, to make hostel life not merely comfortable but luxurious. It was a good thing that the girls' hostels were not as crowded as the men's.

Otherwise she could never have found space for all these extra items, all expensive and in excellent taste. He could see that, despite the dazzling light. Once or twice he squinted into the glare of the sun and wished he had his sunglasses with him. The rest of the trips from the foyer of Helena Hall to the Range Rover were made in silence.

She thanked him shyly as the last of her things were put in the Range Rover. Even the big vehicle was beginning to look overloaded.

'My pleasure,' he replied, smiling, and started to walk away.I'm very grateful.' she repeated. But what about your own things or aren't you going home?' Of course, I am; but don't worry, I can manage on my own,' he assured her. 'I am only waiting until everywhere is peaceful and calm. I don't like all this rush.?

She laughed and then said, 'We don't even know each other's names. I am Mina Erein.'

'Oh, I'm sorry. Richard Pepple at your service,' he said and gave a mock bow.

'Oh — from Rivers too!' she exclaimed in pretended surprise. 'You're a long way from home.'

'So are you, so I don't feel lonely any more!' They both laughed and Mina held out her hand. He took it and shook it. They both said 'pleased to meet you' at the same time and burst out laughing at the for-mality. Richard was about to move off when Mina stopped him.

I've got my car here, can I take you home please?' she asked slowly with a pleading note in her voice, afraid he might refuse.

'I wouldn't want to bother you. Thanks for the offer anyway,' Richard smiled at her, shaking his head.

'Oh please, it's not a bother. I would really love to.

Please, let me. Just to say thank you. You've helped me so much today and I'm going to town myself,' Mina said quickly, her heart begging him to accept.

'All right then, if it's reasonably on your way. I'll just go and get my things.'

Mina went quickly to the Range Rover and told the chauffeur to take her things home. She would come later, she told him. Soon she was driving Richard Pepple in her new blue Fiat 128. Both Mina and Richard did not say much on the drive out of Badagry to town. Richard had donned his sunglasses at last and was watching Mina critically through them.

She was not the most beautiful girl he had ever seen though she had a stunning figure and he admired the silky sweep of her long dark eyelashes. He wondered if her eyelashes were really that dark or it was Mascara at work. He also wondered why he had never met her before. He knew a lot of students in the College, almost all; but Mina he had never met.

Mina was conscious of his eyes on her and when she dared to steal a glance at him, their eyes met. She lowered her long lashes, embarrassed, bit her lower lip and focused her eyes on the road. She concentrated solely on the traffic which was getting rather heavy and tried to forget the man sitting beside her. What a waste of a golden opportunity, she thought. She had dreamed for so long of having Richard Pepple at her side.

Richard could see from the way she bit her lip and used her lashes as a veil over her eyes that she was a very shy person, and was not going to risk their eyes meeting again. She might not be the most beautiful girl but she was certainly very attractive. To ease the sudden tension between them and save her further embarrassment, he decided to talk.

'You are a very good driver — for a lady.'

'Thank you.' She accepted this as a compliment without looking at him.

'I'm going to Ajegunle. What about you?'
'Ikoyi.'

'Well, well, what did you say your last name was? Erein?' She nodded.

'That rings a bell. I'm sure I'm right. You look the part - your clothes, two expensive cars, all the loads - I should have known you are the Ereins' daughter. The fish people. Yes. Yes. Hmm,' Richard said and shook his head. Why did you do that? I mean shake your head? Mina asked him, puzzled. Richard sighed. 'Look Mina,' he said, and glancing sideways quickly at him, I can see you are a very nice, quiet and shy girl, and I don't mess about with shy girls, so I have to be frank with you. We've only just met. We've exchanged a few words and two looks. I like you and I'd like to know you better.

But much as I would love to see you again, I don't think I should even suggest it. You are a rich girl — the only child of a business tycoon. Yes, I know all that, and I am a poor guy. I'm sorry to say, but I have already noticed you are snobbish. I saw the expression on your face when I said I live in Ajegunle. There just can't be anything between us, much as I would like there to be.' Mina was silent. She had not expected such a long speech and it literally took the wind out of her sails. She had known and admired Richard Pepple for a long time at a distance. He had never seemed to notice her, until today, when she nearly fell into his arms. He was active in everything at College. President of one club and an officer of so many others. Everybody knew him. Mina wished her heart did not beat so. She felt sure if it continued throbbing this way, he would hear it.

She had not believed it possible that he would ever notice her, and certainly not sit so closely, or talk to her. She had thought he came from a reasonably well off family. He bore himself so proudly and wore the students'. Mina was silent. She had not expected such a long speech and it literally took the wind out of her sails. She had known and admired Richard Pepple for a long time at a distance. He had never

9

seemed to notice her, until today, when she nearly fell into his arms. He was active in everything at College. President of one club and an officer of so many others. Everybody knew him. Mina wished her heart did not beat so. She felt sure if it continued throbbing this way, he would hear it.

She had not believed it possible that he would ever notice her, and certainly not sit so closely, or talk to her. She had thought he came from a reasonably well off family. He bore himself so proudly and wore the students' 'uniform' of faded jeans and T-shirt with such style.

Many young men seemed more dazzled by her family's name and reputation than by her individual personality.

She had never thought her father's wealth, which had always got her what she wanted, would be an obstacle to something she wanted so badly. She wanted to meet Richard again. She wanted to know him better.

Unable to express her confused feelings, she stared ahead and concentrated on the road.Well, you haven't said anything. Richard challenged her, an amused grin on his face. Mina Erein at twenty-one, was still very young in many ways. The only child of her parents, she was utterly spoiled and nothing was too good for her. Anything she wanted, she got, as far as money could buy it, with a heart shaped face and those long, black lashes that Richard had already noticed could veil her eyes to devastating effect. She was graceful and had very long, black hair.

She was not as experienced as most girls of her age, though she had always had a fair share of boyfriends. Her life had been such a sheltered one. Even now, she still depended on her mother to make decisions for her.At first sight, people thought her to be prim, but on closer acquaintance they became aware that her reserved manner came from the life she had been used to. She was really a shy but most friendly and kind person, once you got through the prim facade.

She was very generous; generous, in fact, to a fault. She spent so much money on her friends. The only problem with her was that she was a snob, as Richard had also observed. It had been subconsciously instilled in her by example, if not by precept, to look down on less wealthy people;

so her friends were from high society, the children of people at the top of the Civil Service and so on. This was a new situation and she had no experience to guide her.

She decided that if Richard Pepple really wanted to see her again, then she had to make it possible for him.

Nothing would be allowed to prevent him, if it has anything to do with her. It was ironic that her family's name and wealth that had always got her everything, should stand in the way of the only thing she wanted right at that moment. She liked this guy so much; oh yes she did; she admitted to herself.

'Well, come on,' Richard was saying cheerfully. 'Say something, even if it's only goodbye!'

She stole a quick look at him. Aloud she said, 'Yes, I'm the Erein's daughter. I don't see what that has to do with it, if you really want to see me again.'

'You don't?' Richard asked, removing his sunglasses and staring at her, his eyes crinkling with laughter.

'No, the way I see it, you either want to see me again or you don't,' Mina said, taking a deep breath before her nerves could fail her. 'Nothing else would matter.'

'All right, can you come out to the cinema with me on Sunday evening, if you are free?' he asked her, daring her to accept.

'I'm free, It's a date,' Mina accepted, elated at her

'What about your boyfriend? Don't tell me you don't have one,' Richard teased.

I'm sorry to disappoint you but right now, I don't have any. You won't believe this, but I'd just finished with all of them. Mina said and they both laughed.

"Well, you are just starting with me.' The strange tension had disappeared and both felt a glow of relief and happiness. They began to talk as if they had years of silence to make up for.

Mina had always watched him back at College and wondered when she would be able to talk to him and what they would talk about. Today, she found out that he was overwhelmingly high-spirited and easy to talk to.

He was the man of her dreams, she thought, and nothing else mattered. She felt at ease with him. He did not make her feel she should be putting on an act as most of her rich boy-friends did. She only needed to be herself with him and she could already see how much he liked her.

By the time they got to Richard's house along Kirikiri Road, Mina knew quite a lot more about him. His parents had both died in a road accident when he was only three years old, and he had been brought up by his uncle and aunt — his mother's brother and his wife.

They also had a son of Richard's age called Douye. Richard had gone to Apapa Baptist School and then on to Baptist Academy Shepherd-Hill before coming to the College. He was twenty-four and his life's ambition was to be Managing Director of a company. He had laughed when he said this, but she knew he meant it. So he was ambitious, intelligent, able, popular, tall, about 5 feet

11 inches and very handsome, with a charming personality too! What more could she hope to find in any man?

Now they had reached the house and the magical journey was over.

Richard did not invite her in. He got out his things and promised to meet her outside the Plaza Cinema by six — on Sunday evening. Mina was a little disappointed when he just got out and said goodbye. She would have liked him to invite her in, or to have found some excuse for them to keep on driving all afternoon. But she felt elated at the thought of their date on Sunday. She drove sedately to the wide roads, smooth lawns.and flowers of Ikoyi with her eyes full of stars.College. Richard waved goodbye, then turned back to the familiar little house. His cousin Douye was gazing after Mina's car. 'Super car,' he commented. 'Supergirl too. Who's she?'

'A friend from College,' Richard said easily. He felt it would be better if his family were to get to know Minan. He did not as a person before they heard she was the Ereins' daughter.

Chapter 2

That first date was marvellous. Though neither of them enjoyed the film much, they enjoyed each other's company tremendously. Richard wanted to know everything about her. They talked about books they had both read and recaptured some funny incidents that had happened during the past year at the College. They discussed practically everything under the sun, from politics to bringing up children.

They met regularly after that, and very soon he took her to meet his aunt and uncle. Afterwards he wondered whether he had been rather too quick - but then, where could they go? He couldn't afford to take her to sit for hours in the international hotels. It wasn't safe to wander about the streets. Once or twice he took her to meet his friend Johnny Marsh but that hadn't been much of a success. Johnny might be in the middle of a session with his rock group or a thunder and lightning with the neigh-bours.

The only time he was there by himself he began joking about their reactions to Mina's car. Richard could see she wasn't enjoying such teasing much so he soon took her away. And where else could they go? So he introduced her to his family. 'This is Mina.' His aunt's eyes lit up at the name from home and he knew it wouldn't be long before she was asking him searching questions.

But for now she was busy making shy Mina feel at home. The love and happiness that Mrs. Daboh could spread around her amazed Mina. Her own mother commanded respect from family and society and gave very little in return. She had never experienced anything like this generous warmth of affection.

It must be a family trait, Mina thought, looking at them all. She always felt very proud of Richard because he was so handsome and courteous. He was particularly patient and pleasant with old people and servants. He had such a way with him that endeared him to them.

Mina learnt a lot about how to deal with fellow human beings, in the first month she'd known him, more in fact than she had ever learnt in her whole life. Richard taught her through his polite and courteous ways that all human beings, whatever their status or position in society, deserved and should be given some degree of respect.

After Richard had brought her home for the third time, he could no longer dodge the questions. That's a beautiful girl, Richard, his uncle said, taking advantage of Douye's absence at a party.

Richard agreed.

'She seems very fond of you,' his uncle added cautiously.

'Very fond!' exclaimed his wife. 'Why, she's in love with Richard. Anyone can see that. And quite right too,' she added with a smile.

'Thank you, you are quite right, my dear. I was just getting there more slowly. What do you think, Richard?

Is she very fond of you or in love?'

'In love..' Richard said rather reluctantly.

'What about you?"

'What about me?'

'Are you very fond of her — or in love?'

"Isn't it too soon to ask that question?'

'I don't think so,' his uncle said seriously; because as I see it, even if you love her, she is more in love with you. Apart from anything else, Mina seems to be a very nice girl. I don't want you to hurt her and it would be so easy for you to do that.'

'Oh!' Mrs. Daboh exclaimed. "How can you say such a thing? Does Richard go round hurting his girlfriends?

He's had plenty but they are poor friends.' 'That's what I mean. Richard is older, more experienced. Mina is probably really in love for the first time. Don't mistake my meaning,' he added hastily, seeing a frown developing on his nephew's face. I'm not pushing you either way, either to love her or leave her.

I am just saying that it would be easy for you to break her heart. I knew you wouldn't pretend to love her when you don't, first because of — well, you know what l mean.'

'1 certainly don't,' his wife declared. "What are all these veiled hints? Just because of something you won't mention and apart from anything else?' She gazed at the two men in perplexity. 'Where does Mina come from?' she asked suddenly. 'What is her full name?'

'She's Mina Erein,' Richard said reluctantly.

'Erein — you mean?'

'That's right. The Ereins' daughter.'

'Oh, my goodness!' exclaimed Mrs. Daboh. 'Oh - dear me! Richard, you really must be careful. Do her parents know?'

'Know what?' he said, rather impatiently.

Know that their daughter is in love with you? Now - don't mistake my meaning either,' she added in her turn. 'As far as I am concerned, any princess would be lucky to be your choice. But if you're not really choosing Mina, your uncle is quite right. Don't break her heart!'

Richard was relieved to hear Douye's cheerful voice in the yard. 'Don't worry — he said quickly. "You're jumping to conclusions. There's nothing serious yet? They quickly broke up the strained atmosphere before Douye could start asking questions. In his heart he knew for Mina at least, the situation was getting serious.

By the end of the holidays when he had to go back to the College, Mina was confident that

Richard was her Mr. Right, and she loved him. He was the man she had been waiting for all her life. She had met and liked his aunt and uncle; they were both very nice people and so was his cousin Douye. They made her feel as if she'd known them all her life. But she had not taken Richard home, for fear that her mother would not approve of him. Her mother's word was unwritten law in their house. Being the snob that she was, Mina thought wryly, she would never approve of her meeting Richard any more.

In the past, she never went to her boyfriends' houses.

As a rule, they always came to her house but this was an exception. This was different. Richard came from a poor family. When her mother 'investigated' him, his background, position and prospects, as she did for everyone of her daughter's dates, what was she going to find? Richard had no great family connections, no land and property, no inherited wealth and position to offer her. Only his love, she thought passionately, and the certainty of the sort of happiness that filled his family's home. The Dabohs might be poor in the material things of this world. It just didn't seem to matter.

So when Richard went back to school, she visited him every other Saturday and wrote him short exciting letters in between, about what she did every day. He never replied to any of these letters - he was a poor letter writer, Richard's excuse, and this was his final year.

After a couple of months, her father began teasing her alot about her mysterious boyfriend.

'Boy-friend?' her mother repeated. That's right. I haven't been seeing Ineye for quite a time.' Ineye! Mina though. Her mother's choice, almost certainly. Good looking, pampered, wealthy— boring. She smiled nervously.

"Come on, now,' her father urged. "Not even a little hint of who and where?' But he wasn't seriously concerned and she could not confide in him.

She despised her own weakness. It was just being cowardly, she told herself, postponing the inevitable because she dreaded her mother's reactions to hearing about Richard. She wouldn't want to know him as.a person. He wouldn't exist as a person, only as a prospect.

She avoided talking much about her parents to Richard too. She knew he must have guessed the reason why she had not introduced him, but he made no comments and so she continued stalling. She kept on writing letters, visiting him, dreaming of the future and waiting for the inevitable to happen of its own accord.

Richard first met the Ereins when he came home for the Easter break. He had not heard from Mina for a whole week. She had not visited him as usual and there had been no letter. He had been so accustomed to her loving routines that this silence jolted him badly. He wondered whether Mina had dropped him — or had her parents found out anything and put their foot down? Or was Mina waiting for him to take the initiative and step into the lion's den of his own free will?

Whatever it was, he wanted to take her to the college's Easter dance the next day. He did not know how to get in touch with her. There was no telephone anywhere around his uncle's house, so he could not possibly ring her. Undecided, he waited until around five in the evening and then made up his mind to set out to go and see her. She worked in her father's firm now and he knew she would be home by six

He set out for Ikoyi on his uncle's motorbike, in a do-or-die mood. He might be doing the wrong thing but anything was better than such uncertainty. He was lucky there was no heavy traffic on his side of the road, as most people were heading towards the mainland at this time of the day. All too soon he arrived at Mina's house and parked the motorbike outside the gate.

No. 21, Coleman Avenue was a mansion, pillared and painted white. Richard mentally doffed his hat for Mina's father. It stood in a wide and beautiful compound and was walled round. On the white gates hung a sign which read 'Beware of Dogs'. That was typical of houses of this type. At the gate was a little kiosk in which sat a security guard in a green uniform.

'Yes, Sir?' said the man, polite but firm.

'I want to see Mina — Miss Erein,' Richard told him cheerfully and was given permission to come in.

Richard pushed the gate back and stepped inside the compound. It was a very big house and the driveway, despite the twin rows of palm trees and flowers planted along it, was as clean as if it had been newly swept. Perhaps there was another security guard, Richard thought, who kept away untidy leaves and stray petals, just as the man at the gate kept out unwanted people. He strode on. He had not anticipated either such size or grandeur and as he walked up the terraced driveway to the house, he mentally doffed his hat a second time for Mina's father, for building such an elephant house.

The first thing he saw as he went in was a magnificent fountain, from which gushed pure spring water. On the walls stood beautiful works of sculpture which must have cost the earth. Here were two lion cubs, one on either side of a lioness; there was a white painted fawn with golden spots. In a corner, surrounded by flowers was a shrine, the Madonna with her baby in her arms. He wanted to step and stare but he felt the guard was watching from the gate, possibly regretting the decision to allow him to enter. Who could tell how many people were watching from the house. He took no notice of the dogs barking from somewhere. He could not see them anyways and went to press the bell.

A maid answered it promptly. He was explaining to her what he wanted when a stout bespectacled woman of about fifty came into the spacious hall. She bore no resemblance to Mina, so Richard did not know she was Mina's mother. She was dressed in an expensive Abada material and her hair was plaited in puffs.

'Yes?' she said, unsmiling and sizing him up with her eagle eyes. A student — jeans, T-shirt and, good heavens, with a crash helmet in his hand. He didn't even have a car!

'Good evening, ma. Please, I'd like to see Mina,' said Richard politely.

Mrs. Rosaline Erein looked hard at Richard and asked him to sit down. She sent the maid to call Mina and continued on her own way, obviously dismissing him as someone of no importance.

Richard looked round the hall which seemed to be used to receive visitors who were not friends of the family. What in the world was he doing with a daughter of such moneyed and sophisticated people? he asked himself. The room in which he sat was very large and expensively decorated and furnished. The stools were made of something very much like ivory, he couldn't be sure, and the chairs were so soft and beautiful, you had a feeling you could sink in them. The table in the middle of the room was made of glass and the crystal bowl of flowers looked like something from a magazine. There was an aquarium at the far end with exotic fish in it.

He longed to go and look at the little goldfish that danced round, swimming peacefully in the water.

Instead he sat stiffly on the velvet chair and stared at the expensive paintings on the walls. Yes, this is class, Richard told himself, with a sigh. No wonder Mina had never invited him to her home. What was he doing here now? The whole thing was a big mistake. He had nothing and everything spelt money in this room. He was still looking round when Mina showed her face over the banisters. As soon as she saw it was Richard, she ran down the carpeted stairs,

'Richard!' she shouted quickly excitedly, forgetting all her fears about this moment. The joy of seeing him so unexpectedly just wiped away every other thought.

Richard's answering smile lit up his thoughtful face.

He held out his hands to her but Mina impulsively flung herself into his arms. Her mother returned and stared, full of unspoken disapproval. Her father, coming in from his study, coughed loudly to announce his presence, but there was a twinkle in his eyes.

'I'm sorry I didn't come to see you on Saturday. I've been ill. I haven't gone anywhere for a whole week now.

Let me introduce you to my parents, Mina said, all in one breath. 'This is Richard Pepple and these are my parents, Richard.'

He shook hands, knowing he was getting a close scrutiny.

How do you do!' Mrs. Erein said, with the coldest formality.

'Can this be the young man who gets so many letters?' Mr. Erein teased. 'We are pleased to meet you, my boy?' He was just a little bit shorter than his wife and was casually dressed in grey flannel trousers and a white shirt. He looked about fifty-five and had a pleasant personality. He was not pot-bellied, like most Nigerian rich men, but he was growing bald. He seemed genuinely pleased to meet Richard, and started filling his pipe as he greeted him. He could see that his wife was not pleased with Mina's choice of a boy friend. He recognised that 'Let me show you round, Richard,' she was saying, with all her attention on the young man.

She was very happy to see him and took him on a tour of her home with the chatter and delight of a child showing another her new toys. On the ground floor, apart from the huge entrance hall, there were two sitting rooms which could be made into one room for large parties. There was a dining room that looked big enough for a conference dinner. All the furniture and fittings were beautiful and in exquisite taste and very, very expensive. Amazed at such luxury, Richard was led to the study, a whole suite of guest rooms, each with its own bathroom, the kitchens, shining spotless, fully equipped with everything money could buy.

Then they went upstairs. One whole wing of the house were her parent's rooms: bedroom, two bathrooms, another private sitting room. Richard's head was reeling. They turned to the other wing of the house. More rooms still! There was Mina's own room, and another large bedroom with a double divan bed. It was clearly decorated for a married couple. Another bathroom!

Then a room with a charming frieze of animals and toys. Then a sitting room!

'Goodness, Mina,' said Richard. 'It's breath-taking.

What do you do with so much space? Don't you ever get lost?'

"You can see I don't use all this yet,' Mina laughed. and the nursery for my baby.

The spare double room is for me when I get married, You mean when you come back to stay for the weekend?' Richard asked, puzzled Mina did not answer and they went back downstairs.

The maid had brought soft drinks and some delicious little snacks to the sitting room. They sat and chatted, making arrangements for the dance the next day. Richard could sense a little apprehension behind Mina's exuberance. He too felt the huge house was full of half open doors and listening ears. He stayed for some time and then went home, after promising to come for her the next evening. Mina walked down the drive with him.

They kissed for a while where only the statues were watching them. Then Richard put on his crash helmet, collected his motorcycle from the security guard and roared away.

Mina waved, then walked slowly back to face the interrogation. Mrs. Erein began asking her questions with disapproving expression. As she heard the replies, the expression grew more intense. When she had finished, there was a painful little silence.

'I am disappointed in you, Mina,' she said. 'You can't be serious. Couldn't you have a better choice?

What am I saying? I don't see how you could have made a worse choice! He's a mere boy still in school. He has no parents. His relatives live in a slum. I can't believe you are thinking of marrying him. What kind of a dowry do you think he can give?'

Now, what do you want with that dowry, mummy? I thought we had more than enough money already!' said Mina in exasperation. 'Anyway, how much is the money? Less than a hundred naira. He'll be able to afford that, don't worry.

Foolish girl, do you think it's the money I'm talking about? It's the name and the prestige,' her mother chided. 'Families like ours marry those of the same status — the same background in society. We don't expect anyone to marry from the slums. And let me tell you, a penniless nobody doesn't expect to marry Erein's daughter! Your precious Richard is just after our money.

'That's not true!' Mina burst out. We haven't actually talked about marriage but I've every intention of getting married to him, if and when he asks me to.'

"If and when!' her mother sneered. 'As if there was any doubt that he would try to marry you and your money. The fellow is just an adventurer!'

'Oh, mummy, honestly! You sound like someone in a Victorian,' Mina sighed, wondering whether to laugh or cry.

'What will our family and friends say, when they hear about this? We shall be the laughing-stock of Lagos society. Ereins' daughter wants to marry a penniless nobody,' she repeated tragically.

"That's their business, not mine. He's not going to be penniless forever,' Mina said angrily, daring to argue with her mother for the first time. She got up and went upstairs to her room.

'Rosa,' said Mr. Erein. 'Leave them alone. You can't choose a husband for her. Those days are past. Mina has a lot of commonsense and Richard looks like a decent young man. A boy who's going to have a University degree behind him, has a great deal of prospects.

She ...

'Spare me the lecture, will you? I knew you would say that. You are fond of heaping sand around Mina's waist. Anyway, I've said mine. If she likes, let her listen to me,' his wife retorted and marched into the kitchen to give the cook orders about supper.

Mr. Erein sighed and filled his pipe again. He knew that he would probably lose the argument. His wife was a very domineering lady, very strong-willed. She had this knack of making him feel always in the wrong. He was very good in his business — that was the only thing that could bring out the iron in him. He was very softhearted about all other things, especially

Mina. He doted on Mina. She had been born after a long search for a child.

His wife had given birth to two sets of twins, one of whom died at birth. After that, there had been no more babies until they had been married for nine years. In the long lean years that followed the death of the last set of twins, members of the Erein family had been on their brother's neck. If he wouldn't drive away his useless wife, then they urged him to take another wife secretly and have an heir. The fact that Rosaline Erein had had twins twice was enough for the elderly members of the family to conclude that she was no good. Twins had been taboo in their hometown and the strong feeling against them was still there.

Ebiowei Erein had withstood all the pressure. He was a Christian and so he accepted twins as ordinary children. It was God's will that the twins had died and no other baby seemed to be coming. He loved his wife and had married her for better, for worse. He could not bring himself to punish her for what was not her fault. He had married her in church, and those days, when you married under the Ordinance, you never thought of taking a second wife. None of them could say anything to her face, anyway.

They were all afraid of her. She could always make them feel so small, staring through them with her big eyes. He smiled reminiscently.

Mina had been born five years after the last set of twins. At first, she was frail and they had thought she was going to die too. They'd nursed her to health as she was very thin and sickly as a baby.

After she'd scraped through the first three years of her life, they knew she had come to stay. After her, there had been no more babies and Mina had grown up to make them proud of her. Anybody watching Rosaline's attitude to Mina sometimes, would think she could not care whether Mina stayed or went. But he, and only very few close friends and relatives, knew that Mina was her very existence. She wanted only the best for Mina always and saw that she got it.

Ebiowei Erein loved his wife and understood her weakness. She had helped him alot in his work:but for her weakness. She had helped him a lot in his work: but for her, he never would have made it to where he was today. People always liked to say-Behind every successful man, there is a woman. In his own case, it was certainly true and he owed Rosa a great deal of thanks. Some people might take her to be the devil in disguise, but he knew that she was a very good kind of wife, very vulnerable too. She might just look angry now but he knew she was really terrified for Mina's future happiness.

He waited for her to come back and then said mildly, 'My dear, have a little more confidence in Mina's good sense. If this young man is the right one for her, one day we shall all agree about it. If he isn't, she certainly feels at the moment that he is. The more you criticise him, the more she'll feel bound to defend him.'

'I suppose you're right, she sighed. 'I worry so much about her.

'Hope and pray,' he urged her. 'I know one proverb says, "Absence makes the heart grow fonder," but another says, "Out of sight, out of mind." ?

Rosa Erein gazed at him blankly. At such times she recalled that her amiable husband was also a cunning businessman, skilled at manipulating others to his advantage.

'You have forgotten Youth Service,' he went on. Young Richard is a final year student. In August and for the next year he will be busy in the NYSC. A little word ensured that Mina was posted here to Lagos to one of my companies because of her delicate health.

Another little word—

His wife smiled at last and gave him a look of genuine admiration. The next day, Mina dressed in a pink floral dress in a crepe woven rayon for her date with Richard. The side of its waist was softly swathed into a velvet drape. She combed her long hair back, pinned it into a bond and waited for him to come and collect her, in this luxurious dress, with elegance in every line of it. As soon as she saw him, she ran out to meet him and they went to the dance in her 128. Any misgivings Richard might have had after his first amazing glimpse into the Ereins' way of life vanished like mist at the sight of her.

It was an all night dance and they had to stay till dawn because it wasn't safe to go into the city during the night. The band played all sorts of dance tunes and the whole floor was filled with young people, eager to enjoy life to the full. Richard held Mina tightly in his arms as the band played a smoothy number, and she felt as if she was in heaven. She wished the band would go on playing that number forever. She had never enjoyed herself so much, really letting herself go for once. In the morning, she felt as weak as all the twelve dancing princesses in the fairy tale put together.

Richard, who didn't feel as tired, did the driving home. He dropped her at her house and stayed for breakfast at her father's invitation. He enjoyed the food very much and did not hesitate to say so. He even praised the cook to her face and that endeared him to her. He was nice to everyone. Her parents were both pleasant to him. Mina felt very proud of him. She knew her mother was making a big effort so she decided not to risk spoiling things by demanding too much. The way everyone behaved showed he was accepted as her 'man', didn't it?

Chapter 3

So Richard went back to College and Mina returned to her routine of writing letters and visiting him. As the examination period drew near, she added good luck cards to her schedule and sent prayers regularly for his success as well as for their happiness. She was so engrossed in her programme of doing all she could do to help Richard at this hectic time that she hardly noticed the increasing number of young men who came on one pretext or another. She treated them all with kind, vague inattention, politely declined dates and forgot about them the next moment.

'That's not the way,' Mr. Erein told his wife mildly. 'I've got to try everything,' she insisted. 'I thought Ineye -

'Mina doesn't notice whether Ineye is in the room or not,' he commented. 'It's a good thing she hasn't realised what you are trying to do. Leave it alone, my dear Rosa.'

'I can't,' she protested, near tears of exasperation Mina had even forgotten about the problem of NYSC posting until quite late. Her own posting had been arranged with no fuss or worry for her. It quite escaped her notice that Richard's posting could be a major problem. So she mentioned it to her father, completely, confident that he would, as usual. He felt quite guilty and luckily she didn't refer to it again Mrs. Erein was still sure that Richard was after the Erein fortunes. One evening, during this period, while he waited for his result, he went to Mina's house, and they were watching television when her mother came in. Mrs. Erein sat down opposite him, cleared her throat like a man and asked abruptly, 'Do you two plan to get engaged, now that you have graduated, Richard?' Richard was floored by this question but he managed to answer cheerfully. 'Yes, of course, ma. I'm still waiting to hear my result and my NYSC posting. I would like to marry Mina as soon as I get a job and can stand on my own two feet.'Rosa Erein reflected for a moment. Her enquiries through contacts at the College confirmed that Richard had nothing to fear about his result. He was sure to get a 2 (1) and might just achieve a first-class. She hid her feelings of satisfaction at the thought of the NYSC posting. 'Yes, a job, of course,' she repeated, 'How do you propose to go about getting that?'

'In the usual way,' he answered, a bit puzzled. 'I'll write applications to various companies and organisations, answer advertisements...'

'As so many people are doing,' she agreed smoothly. 'What do you mean exactly by standing on your own two feet?'

'Being independent,' he said, his perplexity increasing. 'Finding somewhere to live furnishing it -

'That's going to take you quite a long time,' she commented.

Richard agreed. 'Rome wasn't built in a day.'

'But left to you, a job comes first and then somewhere to live and then the means to furnish it to a reasonable standard?'

'That's how it is for most people in this world.' Richard knew he was being gotten but couldn't under. stand how and why.

Mrs. Erein reflected again as if about to bring out some sudden bright idea. "We will give you a job as a Manager in one of our companies with a very good salary. And as you know, this is a big house. We have no other child except Mina. You could get married immediately and live here. If you like, we can convert the East wing of the house into a duplex for you.' She looked at Richard, expecting to see a look of satisfied triumph leap into his eyes.

Instead Richard was shocked and angry. What a nerve they had, he thought, to imagine they could arrange other people's lives to suit their plans. He tried not to let her see how angry he was. 'Thanks for the offer, ma, but I don't intend to sponge on you or anybody else. I want to work where I like and live in a house I choose and pay the rent with my own money.'

'You need not be so curt about it. We are only trying to be helpful. And I insist that, if you are going to marry my daughter, you must work in our firm and you will live in this house. You can see that we've got no son to leave the business to. One other thing, Mina is not going to work anymore, after she is married.'

'But that will be our decision, not yours,' Richard protested furiously. 'It's left for us to decide what we want to do with our married life.'

'I don't know why you should be so ungrateful. This is a great chance that most young men would jump at. You'll be able to save as much as you want to?'

You'll be able to save as much as you want to,' retorted Mrs. Erein sharply, giving him a scornful look, and walked out of the sitting-room.

Richard was livid by now. Most of all he was angry with Mina. She had sat there silently all through this argument without saying anything and he knew she was all for her parents' plan. He wondered why she allowed her mother to run her life for her like this.'Well, she is not going to order me about,' he fumed.

He did not realise he had said this aloud until Mina spoke.

'She was only trying to help and I don't really see any harm in it. They were just thinking of how to make life easy for us. This way, we won't have to worry about bills and things like that,' Mina volunteered, trying to thaw the barrier of ice that had piled up after her mother's exit.

'Will you shut up?' Richard roared, getting up on his feet. 'I haven't even proposed, and you've already laid down such rules for me. Let me warn you, Mina Erein, if this is the way your parents will carry on, you will never find a husband, except of course among your fat-faced socially acceptable weaklings!'

With these words, he marched out of the house, slamming the door behind him. Mina felt the hot tears trickling down her face. This was the first time Richard had spoken so harshly to her, and she knew that unless she made the next move, this was the end of the road for her. She was too shy however to run after him and beg him, so she just sat there crying.

Rosa Erein reported the incident triumphantly to her husband. Such an unreasonable young man,' she added. and quite devoid of any business sense. How could he reject such a splendid opportunity?' Her husband shook his head doubtfully. 'Don't you think you're being unreasonable? If he'd accepted promptly, you'd have felt sure he was after our fortune and position in society. Now he's rejected it, you complain he lacks business acumen. Whatever he did, you'd complain.' I'm not interested in being logical, she laughed, 'I've won. He's gone. That's all that matters to me.

Mina neither saw nor heard from Richard for the next three weeks, and then it was his twenty-sixth birthday. She did not know what to do, she wanted to see him but was afraid of rejection. She confided in her closest friend who was also her cousin. Ebiere's father was a very wealthy man who dealt in carpets and she was about to get married to a young lawyer whose parents were equally rich.

'So he left you just because Auntie and Uncle say he has to work in their firm and live in your place?' Ebiere asked, after Mina had told her the whole story.

'Yes,' Mina nodded.

'What's wrong with that? What has he got to be proud of, anyway?' Ebiere wanted to know.

'It's not like that, I mean...

'And Mina, how on earth did you get involved with someone who lives in Ajegunle? Ajegunle! The things I hear about that place!' Ebiere shuddered and continued. "You won't catch me dead there. Do you actually go there, Mina?'

'Of course I go there, I go to see him and...'

'You go to Ajegunle? Oh Mina, what's so special about this boy?'

'Nothing Ebiere, I love him very much and I want to marry him.'

'You mean you actually love someone who is so poor and lives in Ajegunle?' Ebiere was dumbfounded.

'He comes from a poor family but Richard himself is not going to be poor. He has a degree and will do good for himself.

'Hmmph' Ebiere snorted. 'An unemployed graduate!' 'Ebiere are you trying to tell me that if Muoyo wasn't rich, you would not marry him? Mina asked.

I wouldn't even have given him an audience. Mina, let's be serious. Money is very important in life. You are used to it and you will need it when you are married and start having babies. Ebere advised Mina. You don't know how to be poor.

Mina did not gain anything from her conversation with Ebiere. She had heard it all before from her mother. She would probably have given the same advice a few months ago - before she started going out with Richard. Ebiere did not know better, Mina decided and she was not going to take her advice. She knew she had to see him, and decided to go to his house, since he would be at home. She could leave a message with his aunt if he still did not want to see her. She bought a navy blue silk shirt, and his favourite after shave lotion *Eau Savage* and a card, all of which she wrapped in a sky blue wrapping paper. Then she went to his house, feeling as nervous as a little girl going to school for the first time.

'Mrs. Daboh, Richard's aunt, opened the door, 'Hello Mina! How are you? What a long time since we saw you,' she greeted Mina warmly.

'Come in. Richard is sleeping. You come in and sit down. I'll go and wake him up,' she continued dragging Mina in.

'Oh no, auntie, don't wake him up. I'll just leave his present and go,' Mina said quickly.

"Why? You can't come all the way here, and go away like that without seeing him. Just like that! Even if you are quarrelling today, you must see him and make up,' said Mrs. Daboh and walked briskly into the room Richard shared with Douye, before Mina could protest further. Despite her anxiety about the love affair, Mrs.Daboh had found herself very fond of Mina. She knew Mina and Richard had not been on good terms lately but she did not interfere since Richard would say nothing. She woke him up, told him Mina was there to see him and walked out, before Richard had even got what she said fully.

'Mina?' wondered Richard. 'What on earth does she want?' He put on his shirt slowly and went into the sitting room. As soon as he saw her, he knew how much he had missed her. Did he think he could ever live without her? He was fooling himself. He would want to spend the rest of his life making up for this lost time, come what may.

Mina, on the other hand, could hardly keep herself steady. Her heart was beating very fast. She had this crazy urge to run into his arms, just as she'd done the first time he came to her house.

'Happy birthday, Richard,' she said quietly.

'Oh, so it's the 15th today? I forgot, and so did everyone in this house,' he said easily, 'we're all so busy waiting for the 17th we forgot the 15th has to come first.

Hello, Mina. How are you? Thanks for remembering my birthday.'

'I'm fine, Richard; this is for you,' Mina said, handing him the parcel shyly. Richard started to open it but Mina hurriedly announced her departure.

'So early? Won't you stay and have lunch with us?' asked Richard's auntie when Richard called to tell her that Mina was leaving.

No thank you. My grandmother is coming and we are all supposed to be in for lunch. Richard saw her off to the corner where she'd parked her car. When they got there, he went inside with her and sat on the passenger seat by her side. He caught hold of both of her hands, before she could start the car.

Mina tried to avoid his eyes, and instinctively, lowered her lashes. Mina, thank you very much for coming and thank you for the present. I want you to know that I'm very sorry about how things have turned out. I love you and I miss you very much. But poor though I am, I can't accept your parents' conditions. It would be most unfair of me to ask you to marry me, under the circumstances.

God knows, I'd give my right hand to have it otherwise,' Richard said.

'Oh Richard!' was all Mina said, her long lashes glistening with the unshed tears in her eyes. Then, 'why are you waiting for the 17th?'

'The results are going to be released,' he murmured, putting a hand to her cheek.

'Phone me — please.'

'I promise.' He said goodbye and came out of the car.

She gave him a smile, all sunshine and raindrops that made his heart turn over. He stood gazing after the car.

What had his aunt said — something about Mina loving him more than he loved her? 'I don't think that's true any more — if it ever was,' he told himself.

On the 17th Mina hardly moved a step away from the telephone. The time crawled by. She was seldom busy in the office and that morning, there seemed to be nothing to do but wait and worry and answer the telephone calls for other people. When she had almost given up hope Richard came on the line.

'What are you doing this evening?' he asked brightly.

"What am I doing this evening then? you tell me?

'You're celebrating. We're both celebrating — at the Golden Dragon!" At the Dragon. We must have something marvelous to celebrate.'

'We have — oh, we have!'

'Then tell me' she implored, 'I can't bear it.'

Mina - I got a first,' he said. 'I can't believe it.'

'I can,' she said surely.

'Oh, I love you!' Richard exclaimed. "What a wonderful thing to say: 8 o'clock then?'

'8 o'clock — I'll pick you up.' She waited until he had hung up before she put down the receiver and began to count the hours until 8 o'clock.

They went out to celebrate at a very posh restaurant, Richard insisting that he could now afford to be extravagant on special occasions like this.

They were drinking China tea, unwilling to end a fabulous evening when Mina suddenly remembered.

'What about your posting? Isn't that out too?' Richard looked uneasy. 'Yes — it is. I'm sorry, Mina.

That's not such good news.'

'Where are they posting you?'

'Kano State.

'Kano! Kano!' she repeated. 'How could they do this to us?'

'Look,' Richard begged, 'don't cry here. The Manager will never let me inside again. No more Sweet and Sour Pork —'

'Let's go.'

'Shall I drive?'

Richard paid the bill, then led the way to Mina's car.

'Please.' She sat silently until he said. 'Please, don't take it so hard. I think they delight in upsetting people's plans.'

"I think so too, she said. 'How do you think I managed to do my NYSC in Lagos? A word in the right place —' she felt silent again.

When they got back to Richard's house, his aunt and uncle were out and so was Douye. It was the first time Mina and Richard had been all alone in the house and she went with him to the room he shared with Douye.

She sat on the bed, and he sat by her and put his arms around her.

'Don't take it so hard,' he said again. 'If someone has done this on purpose, they won't achieve anything.

Many waters cannot quench love —'

She agreed, then began to cry. Richard kissed away her tears, then suddenly he was kissing the nape of her neck, her face, and her mouth with a new urgency.

Mina was startled. He had never kissed her like this before. His breathing was rapid and the expression in his eyes was a novelty to her. She was no fool. She knew this meant only one thing. 'But I suppose it has to happen sometime. I love Richard so much. I'm sure I won't regret giving myself to him.' She told herself as she allowed herself to be carried away on the waves of passion.

Afterwards, Mina was so shy that she could hardly face Richard. His expression, when she stole a look at him, was a mixture of love and remorse. He insisted on following her home on his uncle's motorcycle to make sure she reached Ikoyi safely.

At the gate he kissed her again while the tactful night-guards looked the other way. 'No regrets,' he begged her urgently. 'Don't be upset if you don't hear from me for a few weeks. I hear the orientation month is usually in some remote place to discourage stragglers. I'll write as soon as I can and anyway as soon as I get my assignment.

'No regrets,' she repeated and tore herself away. In the shadow of the driveway, she listened to the receding sound of the motorcycle, then slowly made her way indoors.

Chapter 4

Next day it seemed almost incredible that the previous evening had been so momentous — how momentous she realised later when she missed her period. The days passed. It wasn't merely late. She knew she was pregnant. She was not really worried because she felt sure everything would be all right, when she told Richard.

But how could she contact him? She sent a telegram and a courier service letter to his care at the NYSC State Secretariat: 'Urgent message. Please contact Mina immediately and patiently waited.

Her heart leapt when she saw Richard's writing on a hand-delivered letter that was lying on her desk one morning. But it was a cheerful description of the first hectic days in the orientation camp written before he could have had her message. At least she had his address. She repeated the telegram and courier service message and waited again while the orientation month dragged on to its end.

When she had begun to think she couldn't endure the silence any longer, there came, not a letter, but a phone call. At the sound of Richard's voice, Mina thought she might faint. She hastily sat down and cleared her eyes.

'Yes — yes. I'm here. Where — where are you?'

'I'm in Lagos. Mina — are you all right?'

'Yes — fine! Look, Richard. I must see you. Did you get any of my messages?''Fine,' he sounded puzzled at something in her voice.

'Shall I pick you up?'

'No, I'll come to you at 8 o'clock - then the Golden Dragon.'

'That sounds like a celebration,' he commented, a teasing note back in his voice.

I hope it is,' she said to herself. 'See you then, Richard. I love you.'

That evening she delayed breaking the news until she had heard all about the end of the orientation and some of the fun they had had. Then - drinking Chinese tea again — she broke the news. 'Richard, I'm pregnant.' There was a little silence.

'You must have made a mistake,' Richard said in surprise. 'We made love only once. But I suppose that once is enough to... Are you sure you did not make a mistake?'

Mina shook her head. 'No, it's no mistake. I've had a test and they've confirmed I'm about six weeks pregnant. But does it matter Richard? Don't you want this baby?' she asked quietly.

'Of course I do, but I'm wondering what your parents will say. We'll only have to get married sooner - it doesn't matter - we shall go and tell them together now,' Richard said, in all seriousness.

They went together to Mina's house to break the bitter-sweet news to her parents. When they told them, Mrs. Erein nearly hit the roof. She raved on and on, until they thought she would go out of her mind. She had wanted a big white wedding, and a splendid start for Mina in a marriage that was completely suitable. Now, they would have to rush things and the wedding for her only daughter, her only child, would not be as grand as she had anticipated. 'What a disgrace!' she lamented. 'You have let us down so shamefully, Mina.

'Come on Rosa, Mina's not showing yet. She won't show for about two more months, if I know anything.

Surely, you can still have a society wedding, if you are so keen on it? If you start making preparations right away, it will still be grand,' her husband, who took it more calmly, said amicably.

Mrs. Erein took a good look at her daughter and shrugged. She was angry, also that Mina had told Richard before telling her. She had set her heart on Mina's wedding being the grand one she'd wanted, but could not have herself, because her parents could not afford it.

A lot of people still talked about Mina's 21st birthday, and what a huge success it was. She had derived a lot of pleasure from preparing for that party, and had promised herself that Mina's wedding was going to put the birthday celebration in a very dim shade. But now, Mina, aided by Richard, had thwarted her of this opportunity.

It was really Richard's fault, all of it, she told herself. The boy was ill bred, and these boys from the slums, had only one thing in mind. Now he had Mina exactly where he wanted her. She said so bitterly to her husband when they had gone out to discuss the matter privately in his study. 'To give him credit,' she could not help admitting, though a little grudgingly, 'he has stood firmly by her. He knows we could make serious trouble for him and he has no money to get himself out of it.

Her husband agreed. 'Also it's quite obvious he is not after our money. Look at the way he stormed out of our house and never came back until today? He's one of those very stubborn and proud people who have no reason to be proud. She declared.

Well I suppose we shall have to make the best of it. But things are going to be done my way.

When they got back to the sitting room, her husband cleared his throat. I won't pretend to be pleased about this. You have both behaved disgracefully. He glared at them where they sat, hand in hand. Richard, you have your Youth corps to finish.

'But, daddy,' Mina interrupted, surely you can change his posting?'

Mr. Erein thought of all the steps he'd taken to ensure Richard's removal to a remote location. 'No,' he said harshly. 'We will arrange for the wedding to take place as quickly as possible.

Richard with a commanding eye, 'our conditions about your working in one of our companies and living in our house, still stand. You will not be given Mina's hand

otherwise, baby or no baby.

'But that's blackmail. You know Richard will not agree. What are you saying daddy? Do you want me to have a child out of wedlock?' Mina protested.

My only daughter will never have a child out of wedlock. God forbid. Richard will marry you,' Mrs. Erein ruled, 'and accept our conditions?'

Richard did not feel like arguing with them. They had been through all this before. He just got up and went home. Mina got up and ran after him but he pushed her gently away.

' Leave him. He is just trying to call our bluff. He'll be back.' Mrs. Erein said contemptuously.

'How do you know that he will?' I know his type. He won't give up without a fight.' her father said sagely.

Mina believed them. She knew that Richard was a great advocate of legitimacy for children. He believed it to be every child's birth right, to have two loving parents, who were married to each other and loved each other.

Richard told his uncle and aunt what happened and they, knowing how he felt about a warm home life and parents' duties to children, advised him to accept the Ereins' conditions.

Richard refused.

'Do you want to have an illegitimate child? Do you want your child to grow up not knowing his father? I mean not really knowing you?' his aunt asked quietly knowing she was touching a raw spot.

'But auntie, I'll just end up not having a mind of my own. It will be as if they bought me,' Richard protested.

'You love Mina. You want this baby. These are the things you should bear in mind. You should be happy living anywhere with her and your baby,' his aunt said.

'You are Richard Pepple. Nobody can buy you. Knowing you, I'm sure you won't let anybody rule you,' After much persuasion, Richard went to the Ereins and told them he had no choice but to accept their conditions, and so they could go on with plans for the wedding.

Then he went back to Kano, conscious that the Ereins were taking over the arrangements for the wedding and, if he was not careful, for the rest of his married life. What influence could he have, so far away?

On his meagre allowance, how could he afford to travel down to Lagos even if he could get away? Fortunately his primary assignment in a publishing company was so interesting that he could forget his worries for a while.

He was meeting interesting people too, particularly Mr. Wallace, a frequent visitor from Liberia.

The wedding was fixed for a date three months to that day. Although Mina chose to be married in a loosely sewn cream chiffon, despite her mother's preference for the virginal white, Mrs. Erein had no cause to complain.

She gave her daughter the wedding she'd wanted — with all pomp and colour and pageantry. There were lots of flower girls, page boys and bridesmaids, who were all dressed gorgeously.

Mrs. Erein, who was dressed in an expensive kente and beaded blouse, walked up and down the aisle before the service began, leading their very important guests to their seats, even though there were ushers around. All her friends were dressed in expensive kente and paraded themselves about during the reception, all looking so elegant and haughty.

Richard's guests were fewer and less expensively dressed. They looked at the Ereins and their friends' attires in awe and wondered how Richard would cope with such affluence. They felt inferior even though they were dressed in good George materials themselves, and their stomachs churned at the amount of food being wasted. There were all sorts of rich food that they had never tasted in their lives, but as everyone was served by the hostesses, they had a chance to taste almost everything.

They were used to Mrs. Erein's haughty looks, and had made up their minds not to be intimidated by her. During the traditional engagement ceremony most of the Peppies, who had some pride in them, had gone home fuming that day, at the superior airs Mrs. Erein and her people had shown. So they had all come to the wedding prepared not to take any notice of her today.

Mina's new role of wife and homemaker made her so happy that she naturally assumed that things were going well for Richard too. During the first few months they had talked on the telephone, sent letters up and down.

Mina flew to Kano several times and when her mother felt it was advisable for her to stop travelling so much, she arranged for regular plane tickets to be delivered at Richard's office so he could snatch frequent weekend visits.

She did not notice that anything was wrong until Richard became withdrawn and irritated, if she so much as mentioned her parents. One night his eyes, dark and brooding, told her that there was something wrong with him

"What's the matter, darling?' she asked him, cuddling up to him on the sofa in their sitting-room.

Nothing, Mina. Nothing you can help with, anyway,' he replied coldly.

'Try me,' she coaxed, smoothing away the lines in his brow with her fingers.

'All right, if you want to know, it's your mother.

She's always on at me to come to Lagos in a suit and to get a haircut. So I'll fit in better with the family's image — that's the way she puts it,' he told her angrily. 'I have my own image — still!'

Mina was torn between loyalty to her parents and her love for Richard. She knew her mother's sharply critical tongue.

Another thing that always brought about quarrels between Mina and Richard was the number of items bought for the unborn baby. Mr. and Mrs. Erein were always buying clothes and all sorts of expensive baby things that Richard felt were unnecessary. He felt a baby needed so much and no more. Also he wanted to buy things for his own baby with his own money but Mina's parents would not let him.

Whenever he bought anything himself for the baby, Mrs. Erein would explain that it was too cheap. 'It's nice, but wasn't there a more expensive one? I mean something of better quality?' she would ask in the most condescending of tones.

His aunt and uncle had moved to Bomadi with Douye, so he hardly had anywhere to go. He couldn't travel to Lagos and then spend all his time with friends like Johnny Marsh. That would upset Mina and give her mother new cause for criticism.

So in an attempt to avoid clashing with Mr. and Mrs. Erein, he started making excuses to stay in Kano on weekends.

Mina felt a bit resentful, but she could not go there because she was growing very large now. She was never bored. The Erein family was very large and she was still very much part of it. Friends and relatives were always calling to see her.

One weekend, when Richard had, as usual, sent his excuses, her father came in, looking very pleased with himself and so very excited.

'Come on, Mina, and see. I've got something to show you,' she said, beaming from ear to ear.

'What is it, daddy?' Mina asked.

'You just come out and see. It's a surprise.'

'For heaven's sake daddy, can't you tell me what it is?' Mina laughed, getting up.

She had to laugh. His excitement was so infectious.

He took her by the hand and led her outside, all smiles and still not explaining. When they got outside, she found a brand new Mercedes. He produced a set of keys from his pocket and dangled them in front of Mina's eyes for a minute before putting them in her hand.

Then, indicating the back seat, he said, 'Lots of space for children. But daddy, why are you giving me the keys? Mina asked in surprise. Because it's yours. I bought it for you both as a present, her father explained

Oh daddy, you shouldn't have. Mina protested faintly, her heart glowing.

Nonsense, said her father, patting her on the cheek. You know your mother and I haven't given you a very good present since your wedding, so we thought we'd make it up to you. Besides, both your cars are not very comfortable for stretching the legs in. My grand- children will need space to do so. Well, don't you like it?'

Mina flung her arms around him and hugged him. 'I like it very much, daddy. Thank you very much.' Mina could not talk about anything else all day. The mother too was very happy she liked it, and they were all so sure Richard would be pleased. If Mina had any doubts, she kept them to herself.

As it turned out, he was not pleased. He exploded with anger when she told him about it. 'I don't want that car. Your father is going to take it back where he got it from. What's all this, for goodness sake?' he stormed, pacing up and down the room.

'Mummy and daddy think our cars are too small and we need more room for a baby,' Mina tried to explain. 'Shut up, ' Richard shouted. 'Mummy thinks! Daddy this, mummy that! That's all I ever hear around this house. Does it ever occur to you that I might have ideas of my own, Mina? It's a strange kind of marriage when the husband is never consulted about anything.'

Mina closed her eyes and tried to keep back the tears, stinging her eyelids, from falling, but they spilled over and ran down her face as she cried out. 'Damn it, Richard Pepple, I don't understand you at all.'

'That may turn out to be the understatement of the year!' Richard exchanged angrily. 'So little Rich girl, you thought you understood me? Yet you were so sure I'd jump out of my skin for joy any time your father in his great generosity gives me a present? I don't need a Mercedes Benz.

In fact, I don't need any such tokens from either of your parents. I know you cannot tell them, you are too chicken, so I'll do it for you. Your mother already regrets giving her little Red Riding Hood to the Wolf, so this won't surprise her,' he sneered and stormed out of the room.

That was just one of the numerous quarrels they had had over her parents. Mina did not know what to do. Her father would be greatly offended if Richard told him he did not want the car. As for her mother, she would not let Mina hear the last of it.

She already believed Richard thought himself to be greater than he was and she did not like it. If only he could accept their generosity, Mina thought. After all, there was no ulterior motive behind it. But no, it always angered him and turned him into a stranger. She decided to beg him on her knees to let them keep the car, because it would hurt her father's feelings. That would be too bad as the old man had only good intentions in mind when he bought it for them. Richard did not come home before she went to bed.

The next morning, she did as she had planned and Richard was a bit contrite, simply because of her condition, she was quite sure.

'I'm sorry, my dear. If it means so much to you and your father, we'll take the car. But please, from now on, let's make our own decisions about matters that concern us. Promise me you'll tell your parents there should be no more unnecessary extravagant presents.

Mina agreed, happy to have the quarrel over and happy also that he did not insist on telling her parents himself. That would have embarrassed all of them and maybe strained the relationship between Richard and her parents still further. She would know how to put it gently to her father, without hurting his feelings.

But the peace did not last. One Friday evening, Richard flew in from Kano and she met him standing by the table reading a letter. He finished reading it and slumped into a chair.

'What is it?' she demanded, frightened. He looked stricken, sitting down there, his head in his hands.

"That's from Douye, ' he said.

"What's wrong, Richard? Who brought it?'

'A friend of mine. It's my uncle. He's ill — critically ill and in hospital.'

'Critical? Your uncle? What's wrong?' Mina asked, alarmed, Richard's uncle was such a strong man.

'He has to have an operation. I must go and see him as soon as possible!'

Mina put her arms around him, knowing no words of hers could heal the dreadful anxiety that was tearing him apart at that moment. His face seemed older sud-denly. As she was packing his bag for the journey, she suddenly remembered her mother's sister was celebrating her 50th birthday the next day.

She blurted out without thinking.

'It's a shame you'll miss Aunt Lucy's birthday party,' avehing,

Richard flew in from Kano and she met him standing by the table reading a letter. He finished reading it and slumped into a chair.

What is it?' she demanded, frightened. He looked stricken, sitting down there, his head in his hands.

'That's from Douye,' he said.

'What's wrong, Richard? Who brought it?'

'A friend of mine. It's my uncle. He's ill — critically ill and in hospital.'

'Critical? Your uncle? What's wrong?' Mina asked, alarmed. Richard's uncle was such a strong man.

'He has to have an operation. I must go and see him as soon as possible!'

Mina put her arms around him, knowing no words of hers could heal the dreadful anxiety that was tearing him apart at that moment. His face seemed older suddenly. As she was packing his bag for the journey, she suddenly remembered her mother's sister was celebrating her 50th birthday the next day.

'It's a shame you'll miss Aunt Lucy's birthday party,' she blurted out without thinking. As though she had struck him, Richard's face contorted with anger and he snapped at her. 'Is that all you can think of Mina — your family?'

No Richard, I only meant there were so many people I would have liked you to meet and they…

'Always so much and so many, where you are concerned, Well, it's too bad that uncle's condition should inconvenience your plans? He almost spat the words at her before she could finish talking.

'And just what is that remark supposed to mean?' Mina asked, shocked at his bitter note. 'Just what it says. That it's about time you grew up.

You're so damned spoiled that you can't think of anyone but yourself. It's becoming a bore. Believe me, I'm fed up with you and your precious family.'

"Well, if that's how you feel, you needn't come back," she hurled back at him and left his packing for him to finish.'

He finished packing himself. They had both said far too much and there was nothing more to say. The smoke of the brief blazing row hung suspended between them until he left without even a goodbye. Though she knew he would come back because of his baby, she wondered what would happen to them after the baby's birth.

She kept her fears to herself and could not even enjoy the family party that had brought about this quarrel. Everybody asked her what was wrong with her, but she would not tell them because Richard would never hear of her telling anybody about their quarrels.

He came back three days later. His uncle was pulling through. They patched up the quarrel and everything was alright again. The more he stayed back in Kano, the more Mina allowed her mother to fill her days pleasantly with the familiar round.

Four months after the wedding, Mina gave birth to twin baby girls. Everybody was overjoyed, Richard was beside himself with delight because he adored twins.

The girls were not as identical as two peas in a pod, but there was a striking resemblance. Anyone who saw them would know they were twins. When Mina came home, Mrs. Erein was always in and out of their apartment, fussing over Mina and the babies, even though Mina had a maid. She arranged the children's christening with the vicar of her church and then told Mina when everything was ready. Richard saw red and blew his top when he was informed.

'Whose idea is this, that they should be christened on the 24th — that's three Sundays from now? What if I can't get away again this month? There's a Sales Conference that week and Mr. Wallace is coming.

'Oh, is that? I didn't know. Mummy said since it is my birthday on the 24th, it would be ideal to combine both celebrations,' Mina explained.

'Mummy said this! Mummy said that! Oh God, do we have to go by every word or thing your mother suggests, Mina? Don't I have any right to be consulted, even if you agree with your mother? Do we have to lead our lives as your mother's shadow? Look Mina, I'm fed up with all this, fed up I mean. The sooner we leave this house the happier I shall be,' Richard fumed.

'Please Richard, don't let us quarrel over this. I'm very sorry and I promise you such a thing will never happen again, I'm sorry'.

She hated talking about leaving this house. She had known he would be very angry. She herself had not known until everything had been arranged. She had been angry too when her mother told her and had been near to tears at the thought of how Richard would take the news, but however angry she was with her mother she always had her interests at heart and she hated hurting her feelings.

The twins were named Ebibindo when translated fully means God's blessings are now numerous and Toboulayefa, meaning there's nothing like a child! Both these names were given by the Ereins but Richard did not mind.

He got on quite well with his father-in-law, but the cold war continued with Mrs. Erein. She always seemed to know just what to do to annoy him and still make him look at fault.

He promised himself things would be different after he had finished his service year, but in fact, they continued just the same. He now had a well-paid job, a fine office and a company car. Mrs. Erein advised him on his clothes and appearance while he ignored her comments. As a housewife, Mina was not organised.

She was constantly out with her mother and the babies so her husband came back to a lonely evening meal well-prepared by the housemaid. He had to sit and wait until noise and bustle announced that the grandmother had brought his family back.

Mrs. Erein was forever sending them food or inviting them to come and eat at her place, because she felt Mina had too much to do.

They seemed to be always arguing because it irritated him to see Mrs. Erein bustling around doing things Mina or the maid could have done, were they living far away. He knew she needed help. Twins were a handful for one person to manage. He didn't really object to Mina being helped. He was protesting against his own exclusion or relegation to a fringe position of no importance.

Whenever he brought up the subject of looking for an apartment, where they could live their own lives, Mina would refuse to discuss it. She could see no reason why he wanted to leave. They had enough privacy, as far as she was concerned, and her parents did not interfere in their private life. They could save as much as they wanted, since they did not have to pay house rent and such things. They could buy whatever they wanted with their money. It would end in a big argument. She did not realise that her husband was feeling stifled in that house and needed to get out.

The twins' first birthday party had been a grand affair. Mrs. Erein and Mina were all set to ensure their second birthday party far surpassed it. Everybody who was anybody known to the Ereins was invited. There was to be a party for children, between three and seven p.m., and the celebration would go on until dawn for adults, Both Mina and her mother were so excited as if they were the celebrants. They were so proud of the twins because they were pretty children, very bright and advanced for their age. Balloons were tied up high on the ceiling, and there were lights everywhere in the gardens. There were lots of things to eat, drink and take away as presents.

The party for adults was in full swing when the gateman from Richard's office arrived with two rubber dolls for the twins. Richard met him at the door and collected the presents from him. He thanked him and invited him in. He made sure the man was seated comfortably at the table, and asked one of the domestic staff to serve him, before moving off to chat with some other guests.

About ten minutes later, he turned round and found the servant ushering the gateman into the kitchen to have his drinks there. Richard excused himself from the guests he was chatting with and hurried to find out what was the matter. Innocent informed him that Mina's mother had asked him to take the old man to the kitchen, as they were expecting guests who should not be seated at table with the likes of him. Richard was furious and went straight away to Mrs. Erein.

I don't know why you even bother with people like 'Is it a crime to be old and a gateman? What is wrong with that? A thief is more welcome in this house than an honest man. As long as he has enough cash to display, you don't care how he got it,' Richard declared, his voice getting louder as he spoke.

'Please lower your voice. I don't want a scene in front of the guests,' Mrs. Erein said and walked away.

Richard was so mad he did not know what to do. Yet again, he wondered what sort of a woman this Mrs. Erein was. She could always manage to keep cool, when an argument arose between them, while he always seemed to be blowing his top. And the condescending way she talked to him sent shivers down his spine.

All through the party he could not get this incident out of his mind. He decided there and then that this was the last straw and the camel's back was broken.

The next day he told Mina he was resigning and they would be moving out of the Ereins' house. He would submit his letter of resignation that day and he did not care whether he was paid or not. (It was almost payday.).

'But why, Richard?' Mina asked alarmed

'Look, Mina, I don't want any question. I've had enough of this house, and this time we really are moving.

I'm not going to sleep in this house tomorrow night, whatever happens,' he stormed and walked out to work.

Mina told her mother about this and it did not take much persuasion to make her decide her place was there in the Ereins' house. 'Where is he going? What will he go and do? He will have to start looking for work, which is very difficult to come by these days. You will only suffer. It will be like going from riches to rags. You'd better stay here where you belong. You can't leave all these and start all over again. It will be foolish,' Mrs. Erein advised.

'But what if he takes the children? I can't let him go away with the twins like that, mummy,' wept Mina.

'Hush,' said her mother, patting her back as if she was a little girl. 'He will not take them.'

'You don't know Richard, mummy. He will take them away. He said so and he meant it,' Mina argued.

'I promise you he won't. And if you don't go with him, he'll miss you so much that he will come back.' This was her mother's reasoning and Mina was gullible enough to believe her.

When Richard came home, she told him none of them was going to leave that house. Richard told her she could please herself but he was taking his children with him.

'They are not yours alone, mind you. They are mine as well as yours. They are not going anywhere with you.

It's not as if you know where you are going. You don't have a job or a roof. Why should we go with you?' Mina challenged him.

'Oh, you think because I've left your father's employment, I won't get another job? You must be crazy, my dear Mina,' Richard sneered, shaking her.

He was so angry that he packed a few baby things into a bag while she watched incredulously. Then he picked up one of the twins and said, 'I'm leaving one of them for you. I know it will kill you if I take both of them away — not that you deserve my consideration.

'Mina held on to his shirt and screamed at him to give her her baby, it's not safe to separate twins so early in life, she pleaded.

He ignored her

'Richard, just be reasonable. I'll pack both girls' things and we'll all go together.' She clung to his shirt and begged and begged him. Her parents were out and there was no one she could turn to.

Richard was unmoved by all her entreaties. 'You keep Bindo,' he said. 'If it's not safe to separate them, I'll take both of them. I don't want you to come with me.

You've lost the right to do so. God help Bindo so she doesn't grow up to be like you. You can divorce me for desertion or on any grounds you like. I expect your father's lawyer will advise you.'

And with that, Richard walked out of the Ereins' house. Mina, recovering from her daze, cried until she thought she would die, but then she remembered Bindo and her mother's advice and she stopped crying. After all, Richard had nothing with him except the baby's things and probably a change of clothes. He had left everything else he possessed there, so he would come back, she told herself. When her parents returned and heard the story, they agreed with her and the household waited.

Those few things really were all Richard had taken with him, except for his credentials and his passport where the twins had already been entered.

Mina had been planning a summer trip to London. Everything else had been left behind.

To pacify Mina, her parents made very discreet enquiries. There had been no accident to Richard and the baby. They just seemed to have disappeared. Mrs. Erein did not care to have too much noise made over the affair. She still had her daughter and one grand-daughter. She didn't care if Richard had vanished from the face of the earth. For the next seven years, it looked as if that was what had happened.

Chapter 5

Mina got out of the car and walked into the sitting room. The first thing her mother said to her was: "Your daughter's been sulking all day. She won't talk to anybody. You'd better go and see her before she bursts.

Mina sighed. She really did not know what to do with Bindo and her sulks. Mummy, didn't you ask Innocent what happened to her at school?'

'I did but he said, she was so unlike herself today. She wouldn't talk to him at all until they got home. She greeted me, took her lunch and went straight upstairs.

I've been trying to get through but she just ignores me,' her mother explained.

I wonder what's wrong with her now. Bindo is terribly spoiled, you know, mummy. A little girl like her, only nine years old, shouldn't be behaving like a temperamental teenager.' said

Mina anxiously. She took her bay and climbed up the stairs.

As soon as she heard her mother's voice, Bindo leapt off her bed and flung herself into her mother's arms.

'Mummy! Welcome! I'm so glad you've come, mummy!' she cried, as if she had not seen Mina for days.

'Do! What's wrong now? Granny says you have been going about with a long face, as if you failed at school.' Mina teased her, smiling.

Bindo did not smile, No mummy, it's only that there's this new girl in our class called Miatta, She has just come from Liberia and she knows everything. Everything, mummy! She can sing and play the piano.

She can speak English like an American and she can speak French too. And she is pretty. Mummy, they all say she looks like me but she doesn't really. She is

thinner and has such short hair. People can't stop talking about her,' said Bindo. 'I'm fed up.'

Mina smiled. She sat on the bed and Bindo sat near her. She thought she knew what was wrong with Bindo. This Miatta had probably taken over most of Bindo's friends..

'So how does this affect you, darling? I'm sure that Miatta must be a nice girl. Can't you two be friends?' she asked, pretending to be puzzled.

Bindo stared at her mother. 'Friends with that Miatta? Never!' She remembered today at school. She had gone that morning, excited as usual. She was glad she went to a school where there were no strict rules concerning uniforms. She loved showing off to the girls in her class. She had worn a new dress to school that morning and could not wait for them to see it. She found all her classmates gathered around a new student.

This girl was dark-complexioned and pretty, even though she had a very low hair cut. She was smiling and telling the girls something about somewhere when Bindo came in. Bindo's entrance went unnoticed and she did not like this at all. She enjoyed being the centre of attention. She looked at the girl's dress and decided that hers was more expensive.

The girls laughed out loud at something the new girl said and raising up their heads saw Bindo, sulking in her seat in the front row.

"Ah. so you are here Bindo, said Ronke. Come and see your double.'

She's a new girl. You'll like her. She is so clever,' joined Chichi.

Bindo stayed where she was and did not go to them. The new girl moved over to Bindo's seat, and smiled.

Hi! you surely do look like me you know, only Pop likes my hair to be cropped. They've been telling me about you. My name is Miatta.'

Bindo did not smile. She didn't even hear half of what this girl said.

I don't think we look that much alike. You can see I'm far prettier than you are,' she had told the new girl coldly, and Miatta had gone back to her seat.

Bindo's day had only been made when one of the girls told her her dress was fine and then asked if it was new.

'Yes,' she had replied. 'My grandma bought it for me from London.' 'Lucky you! It's beautiful!' came from all corners and then she brought out her packets of chewing gum to share. The new girl did not take any. Bindo was glad her friends were hers again, but when class started, the new girl proved to be very intelligent.

The teachers took to her at once. During music lessons, she excelled herself at the piano and the recorder and also in the French class with her beautiful accent. She could also draw, and paint very well. She had been taught all these by her Pop and his friends in Monrovia.

Bindo, who could not play any instrument or speak good French, thought she would never hear the end of what this Miatta could do. By the time school closed that day, she hated the sight of this new girl and the sound of the name Miatta. She had even quarreled with some of her friends for going around with Miatta or singing her praises. Above it all, Miatta ignored her pointedly though she became friendly with everyone else. Even the boys who called Bindo 'Riche Rich' had no ugly name for Miatta.

'Mummy,' she said now. I can never be friends with that Miatta. How I wish I had a daddy. It was her daddy who taught her all these things she does.

Now Mina understood. She got up from the bed, pulled at Bindo's hand and tactfully changed the subject.

Now now, dear, I haven't eaten all day, can you believe that? I'm starving. Let's go downstairs and find something for me to eat. Come on, smile. At least you've got a mummy. Some people don't have a mummy or daddy, you know,' she told her. Bindo smiled and they walked downstairs together. Miatta, the new girl, was forgotten for the moment.

That night Mina could not sleep. She kept thinking about Richard and Toboulayefa. She had not heard a word from Richard in more than seven years. But for Bindo, she would have gone out of her mind, or have had a breakdown in health at least. A week after Richard left with Toboulayefa, she knew that he would not come back and that she had not done the right thing. She should have followed him. A woman's place was with her husband. If for any reason, he had to go away and live somewhere else, his wife should be able to sacrifice her old family ties and friends for him. But it was on her mother's advice that she had not gone with him. She did not hold it against her mother. She only blamed herself for listening to advice that sounded so wrong now, even to her. Now she was neither a widow nor a divorcee.

She still had a husband. She was Mrs. Richard Pepple, but for all she knew there could well be another Mrs. Richard Pepple somewhere who would be giving Richard all the love and care she had denied him and Toboulayefa, through her childishness. She did not know where to look for him. He did not have many friends and the few she knew could not help her. Nobody, not even Douye, seemed able to tell her where he was. As the years went by, she had resigned herself to the fact that she had lost her husband and one of her children.

She watched over Bindo like a mother hen who was afraid the hawk would swoop down and steal her remaining chick. She and her parents spoiled Bindo.

Nothing was too good for her. Only the best was bought for her. Bindo grew up spoiled, over-indulged by everyone around her. But she was very affectionate. She loved her mother very much and showed it.

Mina always talked to Bindo about her father and her twin sister. Mrs. Erein could not understand why Mina would not forget Richard.

In my opinion, you would be foolish to take him back, if ever he wanted to come,' she often used to say.

'And why do you want Bindo to love him - the father who deserted her when she was only a baby?'

Mina had stopped trying to explain. She kept a photograph of them both on her bedside table and one of the twins on their second birthday. She always had a sad look in her eyes and lived only for Bindo.

Her mother did not see why she was pining away.

She could never stop talking to her about how she should take hold of herself and consider divorcing Richard. Mina would not even think of divorce, until She had seen Richard again. She refused to talk about him to her parents, because her mother was always running him down. On many occasions, when she took Bindo out with her parents to visit relatives, she came home crying.

It made fresh wounds of her grief to see very happily married couples. It reminded her too much of her own loss. Her mother thought this was ridiculous and talked endlessly to Mina about it.

Bindo was not making things easy for her mother either. She had gone to spend the weekend with one of Mina's cousins and closest friends, who had an only child — a little girl of Bindo's own age.

When she was there, she could not help envying Alero. The house was full of love and laughter. She felt lonely and out of place when Alero shared some secret with her daddy. She enjoyed her stay there but was glad to leave. And since then, she had not stopped asking for her own daddy much to her grandmother's annoyance. On her ninth birthday, she had wished for her daddy to come and see her, before cutting her birthday cake.

Even tonight, probably because of the father figure in the new girl Miatta's life, she had asked for her daddy again. It was during the evening meal, and she was merely picking at her food. This surprised everyone because Bindo normally had a very healthy appetite.

No mummy, I was just thinking about my daddy.

Why can't he just come and see us, mummy? Bindo wanted to know.

Mina could not answer, her lip quivered and she stared helplessly at her daughter. Mrs. Erein reproached Bindo and said, 'Now Bindo, don't upset your mummy. I must not hear you asking her about your daddy any more.'

'I wasn't talking to you, grandma. I know if it wasn't for you, my daddy would not have left mummy,' said Bindo rudely.

'Bindo! Don't talk like that to your grannie. Now apologise to her.' Mina said sternly. They all knew Bindo had overheard conversations she was not meant to hear.

'Anyway, if that father of yours loved you, he wouldn't have kept so silent all these years,' Mrs. Erein added before Bindo could apologise.

'How can you say that, mummy? Mina cried. 'You know he loves her. He has stayed away for so long because he never wants to see me again, not Bindo.'

But Bindo said, 'I think grandma is right. My daddy doesn't love me. He would have come to see me if he did.' And she burst into tears.

It had taken Mina over one hour to soothe her, cradling her in her arms and telling her certainly her daddy loved her. There hadn't been many scenes like this in the past but sometimes Bindo would look at her mother and say: Mummy, you are lucky to have a mummy and daddy.

Then tears would trickle down Mina's cheeks. 'You do have a mummy and daddy,' she would say while Bindo sighed with exasperation. Bindo had Richard's engaging smile and quick temper. She also got whatever she wanted and did not forgive easily. She reminded Mina of Richard every day, even though she took after her mother in looks.

The next day turned out to be like the day before. Miatta proved herself more brilliant than anybody thought and she was so nice they all liked her. She taught some of the girls new games and songs. She told them stories about Monrovia and even brought photographs of her friends there to show.

Bindo discovered they had the same surname - Pepple. She was furious and snapped at anyone who said they could pass for sisters. They did not speak to each other and Bindo was sure Miatta was ignoring her on purpose. She complained to her friends who tagged along with her but they could say nothing against Miatta.

Bindo was very upset when she got home. She would not talk to her grandmother and kept snapping at all the servants. The chauffeur who brought her home, said she did not chatter in her usual way but sulked all the way home once again. He was worried because this was most unlike Bindo, who was a chatterbox and suggested to Mrs. Erein that someone went with her to school to see what was the matter.

She usually bombarded him with questions and stories of what happened at school every day. At home she was usually so lively, turning everything upside down before her mother came from work.

'It's a new girl at her school who has a daddy and can do lots of things,' Mina informed her mother when she came home and was told about the problem. "So what is it again, Bindo?' she asked her daughter when she went up to see her.

"Mummy, I must have a teacher. You know that Miatta in our class had a teacher who used to coach her at home,' Bindo wailed.

'She did, hen? Where?' 'In Monrovia. Why didn't she stay there? She's spoiling everything!'

if a teacher is needed. I can get one for you. Stop worrying yourself about this new girl. 'It's a new girl at her school who has a daddy and can do lots of things,' Mina informed her mother when she came home and was told about the problem. So what is it again, Bindo?' she asked her daughter when she went up to see her.

'Mummy, I must have a teacher. You know that Miatta in our class had a teacher who used to coach her at home,' Bindo wailed.

'She did, hen? Where?'

'In Monrovia. Why didn't she stay there? She's spoiling everything!'

'If a teacher is needed. I can get one for you, Stop worrying yourself about this new girl,' Mina said and walked out before Bindo could start on about Miatta's daddy. That's a problem less easy to solve, she thought.

It was around 6 p.m. and the Ereins, including Mina and Bindo, were watching television, when the door-bell rang.

The maid Abigail went to open it and screamed. She ran back into the sitting room.

"Madam, come and see, Oga and the small girl, she cried, eyes wide with wonder.

They all stared at her.

'Which Oga is that?' asked Mina in surprise and then she heard a familiar voice say 'May we come in?' Mina jumped up immediately. She would recognise that voice any day, anywhere. She ran to the hall, her heart-beats thumping loudly in her chest.

She looked at the man standing there unsmiling and it was very difficult for her not to fling herself at him. He was just the same. He hardly looked a day older than when she last saw him. She stared at him for what seemed like hours and could not answer when he said, 'Hello, Mina' softly. Then he lowered his gaze and for the first time, she became aware that he was not alone.

She followed his gaze and her eyes rested on the little girl holding on to his hand. She looked so much like Bindo, only she was thinner, a little taller and looked quite boyish with her close cropped hair. The little girl was holding on tightly to Richard's hand and looking at Mina.

'Is this Toboulayefa?' Mina enquired, looking at Richard. He nodded and Mina immediately scooped the girl into her arms, kissing and fondling her. She was both crying and laughing as she led the way to the sitting room.

'Bindo! Bindo!' she cried. Come and see your daddy and your sister.'

Bindo immediately jumped into her daddy's arms. There was an awkward moment as Richard greeted Mr. and Mrs. Erein. The servants all came to say welcome to him and Toboulayefa. They were all very happy for Mina because they knew it was her dream come true.

Mina could not believe she was seeing her child again at long last. She just held the little girl tightly in her arms.

'Oh, thank God! Thank you, Jesus! So this is Toboulayefa I'm holding in my arms!' she kept repeating over and over again. The little girl felt very uncomfortable and fidgeted to get free.

"Put her down, Mina. She's not used to all this fuss.' Richard said gently. 'I haven't even seen her face properly,' Mr. Erein added. Then Mina put Toboulayefa down for everybody to see.

'You?' Bindo gasped. The other girl too looked quite surprised.

'Have you two met already?' asked Mrs. Eren in surprise.

'Yes,' said Bindo. 'She's the new girl - Miatta - in our class, from Liberia. Remember I told you about her, mummy. For a moment there was a trace of resentment in her voice.

'Miatta?' asked Mina.

'Oh, she's known as Miatta now because she sings like Miatta Fahnbulleh. We hardly ever call her Toboulayefa any more,' Richard explained.

Mrs. Erein sat Miatta on her knees. Miatta sat down quietly and looked around the large sitting-room. She had never been in any room like this before. It was the most magnificent room she had ever seen. Pop did not exaggerate at all when he said they were very rich.

Then she looked at her mother and thought she was very pretty, and very nice too. The grandparents too were not even old. As for that Bindo, fancy her being my sister, Miatta thought.

Yesterday at school, when Bindo had told her coldly that they did not look alike, she had felt as if she had been slapped on the face. She had decided never to be friends with her.

She saw that Bindo was both a snob and a boaster and she liked neither. Miatta had a lot of sense for her age. She knew that without Bindo she could still make a lot of very nice friends at school. She showed Bindo she had no intention of doting on her like most of the girls did and she would not talk to anybody about her.

Some of the girls volunteered information about how rich Bindo's grand-parents were, and what their house looked like. Miatta had not wanted to know.

She did not need Bindo and she did not want to talk about her. And now she was really her own sister?

Hmmmm.

Then Mina started asking her a lot of questions and she had to drag her attention back to what was being said. She answered everything politely in her foreign accent, which everyone liked, while Richard talked to Bindo. Then Mina carried both girls on her knees and started crying again.

'Please don't cry, Mamma,' said Miatta, wiping the tears away from Mina's cheeks with her palms. She felt she would cry too, if her mother did not stop crying. She could never bring herself to watch people cry without crying along with them herself. Mr. and Mrs. Erein excused themselves and went upstairs.

Richard felt most uncomfortable. It was years since he had seen a woman crying. Even though he was once used to Mina's tears, he still felt uncomfortable

because it had been too long since he saw her cry. He wondered why she had lost so much weight and looked so sad. He would have thought she would be very happy at their parting, After all, she had refused to come along.

He tried to make small talk. Miatta did not tell me there was anybody like you in her class, ' he smiled at Bindo.

Bindo, who thought her father was very handsome, told him that Miatta and her were not friends at school, Bindo could never hide her feelings, she always blurted out what was in her mind. Miatta said nothing.

Mina looked at both girls and knew there was no love Lost between them, so she said, "Bindo and you, Tobou oh! Miatta, you two must be friends now. You are sisters so there should be no more quarreling at school."

"Have they quarrelled already? " asked Richard "Miatta started only yesterday.'

He was very much surprised because Miatta hardly ever quarreled with people. When he had asked her if she enjoyed her new school, she had said yes. She told him she had made new friends, so he had assumed that she was getting on well with everyone.

But she had told him there was someone called Bindo Pepple, or another girl who looked a bit like her in her class and that was strange.

"No, ' Mina explained. "They haven't really quarrelled. But they will soon if Bindo continues coming home like she did yesterday and today.

Now Bindo, take Miatta and show her around the house. I want to talk to your daddy,'

The two girls scrambled down. Bindo smiled politely at Miatta and offered her hand. Miatta smiles back, Just as politely. She took the proffered hand and together they went out of the room, Bindo chattering away boastfully already.

"How are you, Mina? Richard asked, breaking the uncomfortable silence that followed the girls' exit.'Just fine and you?' asked Mina shyly.

It was ridiculous, she thought, feeling shy in front of this man, who was the father of her children. She felt as if she was sitting with a stranger and did not know what to say. She was mixed in her feelings. She wanted to put her head on Richard's shoulders and have a good cry.

But then, she wanted to pounce on him, and tear his face to pieces with her hands, for all the agony he had put her through, these last seven years. Richard's answer to her question jogged her back to the present.

'I'm fine.'

'I can see that,' she broke out indignantly. 'You've been doing just fine! So you went to

Monrovia? Straightaway! I thought you'd gone to the Moon.'

'Well, I went to Kano first, to my friends there that I met during the service year. One of the big men - Mr. Wallace - was from Liberia. I told him I wanted a job and — that was it.'

'Just like that.' After a pause she asked, 'Did you contact your uncle and aunt and Douye?' Richard looked ashamed of himself. 'Not directly. I sent them word that I was all right and — well, I told them not to tell you.'

Mina smiled bitterly. Richard's aunt and uncle had sworn to her that they had never heard from Richard.

So other families could also close their ranks against the outsider?

'Oh Richard, you could at least have let me know where you are for the girls' sake. I wanted to come to you but since i didn't know where you were. I couldn't. I could have gone mad with worry, all these years.

Oh, my God —' Mina said brokenly, with tears in her eyes.

'But you made it so plain you would not leave this house,' Richard said coldly.

That was seven years ago. Did it never occur to you that I could have changed my mind over the years or that I would want to see my daughter?' Mina protested, but Richard said nothing.

She did now know what to do. She had stopped putting a name on her feelings for him long ago. Now that she saw him again, she felt a mixture of love, desire and hate for this man who had treated her so cruelly. She knew he was like the elephant, who never forgives or forgets easily; but seven years! Oh God, she could kill him for the hell he had put her through.

'Richard, you went too far, keeping silent like that all these years. You knew where I was and yet you didn't get in touch at all,' she said, shaking her head. Tears trickled down her cheeks.

'Mina, a wife's place is with her husband. You thought yours was with your parents. You were still too tied to your mother's apron strings. You were not ready to start a real home with me.

What was I to write to you about? Miatta? She was getting on well without you and...'

'Didn't you ever wonder about Bindo? If you did, you would know I worried about Tou... Miatta, Mina protested.

'Mina, can we change the subject for tonight? We can talk about this some other time. I guess I owe you an apology. It can't be easy for you to forgive me but try to.' Richard said.

Mina became silent. He was right. Tonight was not the night to sort this out. This was a time of rejoicing.

She did not know what to say next. She knew even the admission that he was wrong at all must have cost Richard a lot.

Richard wondered again why Mina had that sad expression on her face and why she was com expression on her face and why she was so much thinner.

The Mina he knew had never been fat but had always had that aura of contentment about her. This Mina was like a woman who carried all the problems of the world on her shoulders, with the far away, sad look in her eyes. He kept looking at Niobe and felt sorry for her. Conscience began to prick him.

Mina turned her head and caught him looking at her. Embarrassed, she gave a little laugh and said, 'Oh, I'm sorry. I haven't asked you what you will take. Do you want anything to eat or drink?' She was confused and knew she had not put the offer nicely, but pray, how was she to talk calmly as if nothing had happened?

'No, thank you,' said Richard, shaking his head.

'Richard, do take something, please,' Mina pleaded.

Richard did not feel like taking anything, but he could not help consenting to a bottle of Coca Cola, because of the pleading look in her eyes.

'Is that what you take now?' she asked, as she went to one of the shelves to bring out a photo album for him.

Richard replied that he was watching his weight and had stopped taking alcohol. He did not want to have a big tummy.

'But soft drinks are all sugar,' she said seriously and then burst into laughter. What sort of stupid conversation was this? 'You haven't changed at all.'

'That's more than I can say for you?' Richard said, taking the album from her.

The big album was marked Bindo. It contained photographs of Bindo's growing stages over the years.

Richard leafed through the pages. He had a feeling akin to nostalgia at Bindo's smiling face, as she posed for the camera each time, reminding him he had missed so much of the growing years of the little girl. He was very happy Mina had kept such a good record of Bindo;s life and achievements. He had similar things of Miatta and made a mental note to bring them along for Mina to see next time.

'You've finished showing her around?' Mina asked Bindo. Both girls nodded. Miatta looked a little dazed.

'It's a beautiful house. Sure is, Pop! You should see the whole house and Bindo's room. It's so big, and Bindo... she got some heaps of toys and things!' Richard agreed solemnly that he was sure she had.

'Mummy, I gave Miatta one of my dolls and a sewing machine. She said she liked them, but she wouldn't take them,' Bindo told her mother.

Mina looked enquiringly at Miatta, who glanced swiftly at Richard and looked down at her toes. I only meant they were nice. I don't really want them,' she said in her lilting voice.

Mina looked at Richard.

He shrugged and said comfortingly. 'That was very kind of you, Bindo. But Miatta is not used to taking things unless she asks me first or she is particularly close to the person who gives her.'

Mina smiled and pulled Miatta into her arms. She loved this little clever girl very much. She could see that Miatta had a lot more sense in her head than Bindo had.

Bindo would have thought nothing of accepting things and showing them to her mummy later. Or was Miatta just like Richard, finding it difficult to receive anything graciously?

Miatta still would not take them, even though her father said she should. She had her own toys and did not really want more, she insisted. She had only praised them. Small though she was, Miatta had a lot of sense.

She had no intention of taking things from Bindo, just in case Bindo went to school and bragged to everyone.

Mina asked her if she wanted anything to eat but she said no. Mina looked helplessly at Richard, who told her not to worry. Bindo's album was given to Miatta to go through and when she finished, Richard stood up and said it was time they went home.

'Oh daddy, can't you stay here tonight?' wailed Bindo. 'No honey, we have to go now but we shall come to see you again soon.' 'Oh, but mummy, I thought we were all going to live together now. I don't want us to be apart any more.' Bindo cried, clinging to Richard's hands and looking pleadingly at Mina.

Miatta just stood there, looking starry eyed at them. She knew that she would have to go home, if Pop did not want her to stay. She knew her father very well. He rarely went against his decisions or had his mind changed for him by other people.

Richard, can't Miatta stay for the night, please?' asked Mina. She knew how Bindo was feeling because that was the way she felt too. She had half hoped that Miatta would stay with them for some time before Richard finally got himself settled.

'No, I mean, I didn't come prepared for her to stay. She can come on Friday and stay for the weekend. And maybe we could all go out to the Bar Beach or somewhere on Saturday. Miatta hasn't been anywhere and she would love to, said Richard determinedly. He murmured, it's been a big surprise to both of them. Don't push it too far.

Fine, that's alright then, Mina said. Her parents came down and there were restrained goodbyes.

Mrs Erein apparently had felt like Bindo and was sad when she was told Miatta had to go. They all looked forward to Friday, when she would be coming back.

On the way home, Miatta was very quiet. She kept her eyes glued on the window on her side of the car. Looking out into the darkness, at the streets. She thought of how much she would have loved to stay.

Richard glanced at her, Happy? He asked her. Miatta smiled and nodded.

You would have loved to stay. Wouldn't you?

Miatta was surprised at this question. She did not know what to answer. She glanced quickly at her father's face and saw the twinkle in his eyes. She knew it was safe to say whatever she felt, so she nodded again.

Already thinking of leaving your Pop, are you? So as soon as you see your mummy, you want to desert me for her? He joked.

Oh no Pop, It's only that I'm so glad to see her. She's so nice and pretty.

Yes, your mummy is a nice woman. She was even prettier than she is now, you know, Miatta. Now she looks sad.

Yes pop, Bindo told me that she always cries for you and me, and that she'll be very happy now. Pop I wish we could all live together now, Miatta said.

Richard patted her head , smiled and said, we will see about that, honey. Why didn't you tell me Bindo was in your class?

Pop, I didn't know Bindo was my sister. She snubbed me yesterday, so I said I won't be friends with her. I never even knew her surname was Pepple, because I don't allow anyone to talk to me about her.'

'Is that so?' Richard smiled. 'What about your grandparents? What do you think about them?'

'They're nice too. They talked to me a lot, especially grandma. She wanted to hear all about Monrovia and all our friends there,' Miatta said excitedly while Richard hid a smile at the thought of Rosaline Erein starting her investigations once again.

All night, Bindo talked of nothing else but her daddy's visit. She was so excited she could not sleep. She kept on telling her mother how happy she was.

'Oh mummy, when can we go and stay with them? All our class girls will be surprised tomorrow to know that Miatta is my sister. I shall never ever quarrel with her again.' She went on and on and refused to stop talking even when her mother threatened to punish her.

'Mummy, are you glad Miatta is back?' she whispered to Mina. 'Yes, I'm very very glad, darling. It's the best thing that has happened to me for a very long time. It's my greatest prayer that has come true for you both to know each other.'

'And what about daddy? Are you glad to see him?' Bindo asked her.

'Of course I am,' smiled Mina.

'Will you still marry him?' Bindo wanted to know.

'Bindo! Go to sleep. There's school tomorrow, you know.'

'Please, tell me mummy!' Bindo persisted.

'Maybe, Bindo, maybe,' laughed Mina.I never stopped being married to him, you know.? "Goodnight, mummy,' smiled Bindo and closed her eyes.

'Goodnight Bindo darling, 'said Mina, laughing. Whatever gave Bindo such thoughts, she wondered.

Children learn too much very early these days. Imagine a little girl only nine years old and asking such adult questions. Bindo was fast asleep now. She always was, as soon as her head touched the pillow and she closed her eyes. But Mina knew that the next day there would be a whole lot of new questions to be answered. Then there was her mother, who was dying to know what she had settled with Richard, if anything. Mina had just managed to ward her off with a tired yawn and had come up to bed immediately.

The next day, Bindo got to school before Miatta. She told all her classmates that Miatta was her twin sister, Tobouleyefa, and she had come to their house with their daddy. They were friends now and they were never going to quarrel ever again.

The whole class was surprised. "Is it true? You don't really mean it, Bindo!' they all gasped, one after the other.

'Well, didn't I say she's your double?' Ronke laughed. Bindo ran to meet Miatta and hugged her, when the latter arrived. Did daddy bring you? asked her sister. Yes, replied Miatta. He is waiting outside to see you.

Come on, Leave your bag and let's go, said Bindo, dragging Miatta. She could hardly wait to see the surprise on her friends faces when they saw her daddy so she gave Miatta no chance to say hello to the others. She took Miatta's bag from her, dumped it on her own desk and dragged her outside. so she gave Miatta no chance to say hello to the others.

She took Miatta's bag from her, dumped it in her own desk and dragged her outside. Bindo jumped into Richard's arms.

'Hello and how are you this morning?' he asked her, hugging her. 'I'm fine daddy, thank you?' 'And how is your mummy?'

'She's fine too. She will be coming to take me herself this afternoon so that she can see Miatta,' Bindo informed him.

'Say hello to her then,' smiled Richard. 'Anyway I shall see her tomorrow. I have to go now.' Miatta turned around and found that they had an audience. Nearly all the girls in their class and a few of the boys were watching them. They were all introduced to Richard who shook hands before leaving.

Bindo quickly told their teacher of her relationship with Miatta and the teacher was very happy to hear the good news. She wasn't particularly surprised.' This was sophisticated

Lagos and many of the children had complicated family lives.

Throughout that day, they were seen walking around hand in hand and soon the news was all over the school.

They both flew into Mina's arms when she came in the afternoon, and her heart warmed towards both of them when she saw them together. Yet again she sent a silent prayer of thanks to God.

They all stood and talked for a long time until Miatta had to go with the driver her father had sent. Although she was sad to leave her mother and sister, Miatta waved goodbye without a frown, knowing she would see them tomorrow,

Chapter 6

Mina found herself taking more time than usual with her dressing. She pretended she could not understand why she wanted to look extra special, when she was only going to the school. That was almost an everyday routine. She nearly always took Bindo to school in the mornings, except when she was already late for work.

She would not admit to herself that it was because of Richard. She refused to analyze her feelings for him, even to herself. Her mother had asked her several times in the past couple of days what they intended to do now but she had no answer to any of these questions.

She got to the school a little before closing time, and found Richard waiting. They greeted each other casually and waited in silence for the girls. Richard leant against his car and watched Mina. He was surprised to see there was a visible change in her since Wednesday. She looked relaxed and happy already. Looking at Mina,

Richard understood why people say beauty comes from within.

When you are happy, you will be beautiful. The hustle and bustle of children coming out of their classrooms jogged him out of his thoughts abruptly.

'Did you enjoy school today?' Richard asked his daughters.

'Yeah, Pop,' Miatta said and Bindo nodded. "Well then,' said Richard, opening the car door and bringing out Miatta's little overnight case. 'Here are your things, Miatta. I only came to say bye bye?'

'Thank you, Pop,' said Miatta, taking the bag from him.

Now, behave yourself or you won't be allowed to go there any more, ' Richard said.

'Don't worry, Pop. I'll behave,' Miatta told him with a smile. 'Oh Richard, did you have to say that?'

'Daddy, when will you come and see us again?' Bindo asked, feeling left out.

I was thinking of taking you to the Bar Beach tomorrow, but I hear there's a new Amusement

Park at Apapa. Miatta has never been to one. So if it's alright by mummy, I'll come and take you all on Sunday,' Richard said, looking at Mina.

'It's all right but make it in the afternoon,' Miatta said quietly, with a smile.

'Why do you both talk to each other as if you are strangers? Alero's mummy and daddy don't behave like this. They kiss and laugh. Why can't you be like that too?' Bindo quipped.

Both Mina and Richard were embarrassed. 'Bindo!' Mina exclaimed in amazement. 'It's true!' Bindo stated stubbornly.

'Look here, honey. What do you know? Children shouldn't say things like that. They are not meant for you to say.' Richard scolded her, bending down and holding her by the shoulders.

Bindo moved away from his grip, sulking and stood on her own.

Richard ignored her, said goodbye, got into his car and drove off. Bindo climbed into the back seat of her mother's car as soon as the driver opened the door. "You don't have to like him, you know,' said Miatta, on the defensive, 'If I were you, I'd think twice before saying things like that.'Miatta waited and was going to open the front passenger door when her mother stopped her. "Don't you like sitting at the back, Miatta?'

"I don't mind sitting anywhere, only I got used to sitting in front with Pop.'

'Come on and sit with us at the back then.' Mina invited her.

Mina looked at Bindo and was not surprised to see her still sulking. She took hold of her hand and said:

'Bindo, you shouldn't say things like you said the other time. You embarrassed your daddy and me very much, you know. Children are not supposed to pry into older people's affairs."

'Why?' demanded Bindo. "It's true, and I don't think I like daddy very much. He was angry just because I said that.' 'You don't have to like him, you know,' said Miatta, on the defensive, 'If I were you, I'd think twice before saying things like that.'

'It's no business of yours what I say, Miatta!' "You are spoiled, that's why,' Miatta said with a grin. Mina could foresee a quarrel in the making. It amazed her the way Miatta sprang to Richard's defence. She could see that she would have a

124

hard task trying to get these two to forget that. they had been living with different parents nearly all their lives. She sighed sadly.

"Now both of you, I don't want you to quarrel. Bindo you have to admit it when you are wrong. And next time, just let things be. Don't ask unnecessary questions, okay?' Mina said, stroking Bindo's head.

'Okay, mummy, I'm sorry." 'I'm sorry too.' Miatta said, smiling at her sister.

Bindo smiled back and they were friends again. That night at home, Mr. and Mrs. Erein made a great fuss over Miatta. She sang and played the piano for them.

They were delighted with her and gave her lovely dresses they had bought for her. Miatta was thrilled and ran upstairs to show the dresses to her mother.

"They are lovely. Did you say thank you?' Mina asked her.

'Oh yes!' said Miatta excitedly. 'Oh mama, they are nice, aren't they? Please say thank you to them for me. Pop always does.'

'Okay Miatta,' smiled Mina. 'But they are my parents you know and they are free to buy you things, darling.?

She took Miatta's hand and went to thank her parents. They all had a nice evening and when it was bedtime, both girls climbed on Mina's double bed.

'I'm very happy to be with you and mama. Miatta whispered to Bindo. 'And I'm glad you are here,' Bindo replied.

The next morning Miatta wanted to eat something her mother had cooked. So Mina prepared breakfast for them and took them out shopping. They went to the Falomo Shopping Centre and roamed about there, buying this here and that there. Miatta was thrilled with everything and exclaimed delightfully at all her mother bought for her. When they got home, they found Mr. and Mrs. Erein had visitors, an elderly couple.

Bindo flew into the bespectacled lady's arms. 'Surulere mama!' she shrieked in joy. The lady hugged and kissed her before putting her down.

Mina dragged Miatta forward and introduced her. 'Surulere Mama, this is

Toboulayefa,' she said. Surulere Mama nearly fell over in her rush to grab and hug Miatta. She was Mrs. Erein's sister Lucy and had been nicknamed Surulere mama by Mina because, ever since Mina could remember, Auntie Lucy had been living in Surulere. Tears of joy trickled down her cheeks as she hugged and hugged Miatta tightly to her bosom.

"So how are you, my child?' she asked Miatta.

'I'm fine, thank you, ma.'

'Miatta, that's grandmummy's sister, so she is your great-aunt,' Mina informed her. "And that's her husband.'

Good evening, sir,' Miatta smiled at him.

Now girls, go upstairs and tidy yourselves up. You are as dirty as piglets,' said Mina, showing them up-stairs.

"What a pretty, well behaved girl she is,' commented Lucy's husband as the girls went out.

'Oh yes, she behaves far better than Bindo, I must say, Richard had done a very good job of bringing up Miatta, seconded Mina's father.

'How come she's now Miatta?' Surulere Mama asked.

"You should hear her sing, then you won't need to ask,' Mrs. Erein laughed. Her father says she sings like Miatta Fahnbulleh — that Liberian singer.'

'So, Mina, do you intend to get together again now that Richard's back?' her aunt asked.

'I don't know yet,' said Mina. 'We haven't talked about it.' 'You don't have to agree as soon as he asks you, you know,' said her mother.

'Well, why not? She doesn't need any coyness with him. After all, they've got those two up there to consider,' objected Surulere Mama.

I know and I'm not saying she should refuse. She should be able to restrain herself a little or he'd think without him she cannot live. Just look at the way he walked out on her!

In my own opinion, she's had good grounds for a divorce, said Mrs Erein sternly. 'But I didn't want a divorce and I still don't. And as soon as he asks me to come back, if ever he does, I'll say yes. But for now, he hasn't, so let's forget it,' Mina said, surprising even herself. She didn't know where the words had come from.

They changed the subject and talked about the resemblance between Bindo and Miatta. Surulere Mama was so happy for Mina that she kept praising God. The visitors stayed to eat supper with them. While they were eating, Bindo started telling her grandparents about the things they had done that day.

'Bindo, don't talk with your mouth full, Mina scolded.

"She always does,' said Mrs. Erein.

'No,' I don't!' objected Bindo.

'Yes, you do, because you are spoiled. You have no manners,' said her grandmother again.

Miatta thought this was a joke and Bindo, upset, got up from the table and stormed off to the sitting room.

Mina was upset with herself. It always worried her when people called Bindo a spoiled child. She knew Bindo could not help being what she was and she always felt as if the rebuke was aimed at her. Bindo always got upset and very difficult to console when she was referred to as a spoiled child.

'Did you have to say that, mummy, and when she was eating too? Now, she won't want her food any more,' she reproached her mother wearily.

'Don't worry, I'll go and get her,' offered her father. He went to the sitting-room where Bindo was sulking on a chair and lifted her up. 'Come on, my dear, don't mind grandma. Come and finish your food,' he told her, tickling her.

Bindo did not smile. 'Grandma just loves upsetting me, and that Miatta had to go and laugh, just because everybody's making such a fuss of her. Why do you all treat her like she's a princess?' she demanded.

Her grandfather put her down and turned her around to face him. 'Well, you know for over seven years, we didn't see as much as a photograph of her. It's only natural for everyone to treat her like that,' he explained to her. 'And she is such a good girl, like you. You don't have to be jealous of her. You know we all love you very much but she doesn't know how we feel about her. We have to show her that we love her too.

Now, are you coming with me?

Bindo nodded and smiled, pleased that her grandfather had said she was a good girl. He took her to the table and she finished her supper.

'What's the matter with you, Miatta? Didn't you enjoy your day with us?' Mina asked worriedly, noticing that Miatta had kept very quiet since they finished eating.

'Oh no I did, very much, mama. I was only thinking about poor Pop, all alone at home. He always had me with him. I'm sure he's terribly lonely. I wish we had a telephone at home so I could talk to him,' Miatta said, much to the surprise of everyone.

Mina smiled and shook her head. 'I'm sure your father is all right. You'll see him tomorrow,' she told the little girl.

'I know, mama,' Miatta said quietly. Miatta, why can't you say mummy and daddy instead of mama and pop?' Bindo asked.

I could, but I'm used to mama and pop. Andy and Sandra call their parents that and that's what I call them too?' 'Andy and Sandra Wallace. Their father owns the company pop works in. They are black Americans and they lived in Monrovia but now Sandra and Andy have gone to school in Philadelphia. Their pop and mama are still in Monrovia,' Miatta explained.

Were they the ones who took care of you when you were a baby? Bindo asked.'Yes, Pop said Mama did until he got Mamee - she was my nurse. Mamee is a Liberian and she taught me to speak Kru and so many of the songs I know. I used to go to music lessons with Sandra and Andy, that's where I learnt to play the recorder and piano,' Miatta told her. 'Were they nice to you?' Bindo asked again.

They all were. I liked it very much there.'

'Better than you like it here? Mr. Erein teased I don't know. Lagos is so big but Monrovia is small.

I wanted to come to Lagos and see you all. Sandra and Andy could not stop talking about going to America so I told Pop I wanted to come here and he said okay. And we came.' She finished as the telephone began to ring.

Bindo picked up the telephone.

'Hello, is that Bindo?' The voice on the phone asked.

'Yes. Who's that?' she asked.

'Daddy, the voice on the other end laughed

'Daddy! We were just talking about you,' Bindo cried excitedly. She closed the mouthpiece with one hand and called to her sister. 'Miatta, it's daddy!' Miatta got up and ran to the telephone.

'Daddy,' Bindo was saying as Miatta got there, 'we went shopping today and... Hold on, Miatta wants to speak to you.' She handed the receiver to her sister.

'Pop! Hi! Where are you phoning from? Are you all right?

Did anybody come to stay with you?'

'Hey steady on girl. One question at a time! Her father laughed. 'Of course, I'm alright and I'm enjoying myself you know. I'm phoning from a friend's house. There's a party going on here. Then to your third question, nobody came to stay with me. I'm not a baby. Right?'

'Right Pop!' Miatta laughed too. 'Pop, we went to so many places today. Oh, please say thank you to mama and grandma and grandpa for me. They bought me lots of things,' Miatta chatted excitedly.

'That was very kind of them, 'said Richard dryly. Is your mama there?'

'Yes — Bindo, call mama,' Miatta said. 'Pop, are you still coming to take us out tomorrow?'

"Yes. Can I speak to your mama now?'

'All right,' said Miatta, giving the receiver to her mother.

'Hello Richard. Where are you phoning from?' Mina asked quietly.

'Hello, Mina. From a friend's place. You should remember him — Johnny Marsh?'

I know him very well. So he is still in this city,' Mina said, amazed that Johnny was still in Lagos. Funny that she had seen so little of Richard's friends since their separation.

'Yes, he is very much around and there's a party going on here,' Richard's voice came from over the line.

'Mina, thank you very much for the things you bought for Miatta. And please thank your parents too. You needn't spend so much on her, you know?'

'For heaven's sake, Richard! Miatta is my daughter as well as yours,' Mina said in exasperation. "You don't have to thank me for buying her anything. Anyway, are you still coming to take them to the Amusement Park tomorrow?' "Yes," replied Richard. I thought you'd be coming with us too. That is if you haven't got anything else lined up?"

Mina thought for a moment before answering, even though she had nothing else planned. 'Yes, I'd love to.

Thank you, Richard.'

'It's nothing, I just rang to see that Miatta was settling down fine. It seems as if she is. When can I come for you? 4 p.m. alright?'

'Fine. Richard, I'm very sorry about what Bindo said yesterday. I know, it embarrassed you but that's just Bindo. She doesn't mean any harm, really. Only she is rather impulsive and outspoken. She doesn't know that it hurts at all?' Miatta apologised on Bindo's behalf, talking as fast as she could.

"Don't let that worry you, Mina, Richard said. "You were more embarrassed than I was. I think that girl needs a little discipline. I bet all you give her is love.

Anyway, she's my daughter, so I shall have to adjust, won't I?' he asked and laughed,

Mina laughed too and he went on. I have to hang up now. Are they there?'

"Yes, they are both right behind me here. Good night Richard,' Mina said. She handed the telephone to Bindo, who chatted brightly with Miatta butting in now and then.

A few minutes later, she gave it to Miatta.

'Okay pop, ring off now or your friends will have to pay lots of money, won't they? Bye,' she said with the wisdom of an adult.

Richard laughed, pleased at her thoughtfulness. It always amused him whenever she spoke or behaved like a grown up. Miatta was too clever and too thoughtful for her age.

She would make a very formidable old lady. 'Bye Miatta,' he said. 'See you tomorrow. Let me say bye to your sister.'

Miatta gave the telephone to Bindo who said goodbye to her father. And Richard rang off at last.

Chapter 7

After church, when the girls joined her, Mina was talking to a young man she had known long before she ever met Richard. Ineye was the son of Mrs. Erein's best friend and he had been friends with Mina all her life.

He was her very first boy-friend, and the two mothers had been very busy match-making. As soon as Mina met Richard, Ineye had been quite eclipsed. After Richard left, he had tried to get back on the old footing with her, but Mina would not allow it. She kept any contact firmly casual and merely friendly.

Today, he looked disheartened as Mina told him her news.

'Uncle Ineye,' quipped Bindo, 'my daddy is back.'

'So I hear,' smiled Ineye, with an effort.

Bindo pushed Miatta forward and said: 'This is my sister Toboulayefa, but we call her Miatta.'

Ineye shook Miatta's hand. 'How are you? I'm pleased to meet you, Miatta.'

'I'm fine, thank you sir,' Miatta smiled shyly and went to hold her mother's hand. "We are all going to the Amusement Park this afternoon, Uncle Ineye. Are you coming too?' asked Bindo, head on one side.

'No, I'm afraid not. I am not a member of your family so you won't want me,' Ineye said, amused. announced, Okay, I'm taking Miatta to the pastor, Bindo announced, no more interested in Ineye.

'Go on then. I'll meet you there,' Mina said, "You've got quite a job cut out for you, Mina, Ineye watched them go.

'Are you telling me?' Mina laughed along with him,

'They are so different. Miatta seems quieter than chatterbox Bindo. You have quite a handful there.'

'Oh yes. She's as full of life as they come, that Bindo, but don't be fooled. Miatta has a mind of her own,' Mina agreed with him, walking towards the Parsonage.

Ineye caught hold of both her hands. 'Mina, I suppose now that Richard is back, I will mean nothing to you anymore?' he asked her solemnly, looking straight into her eyes.

Mina drew her eyes away from his gaze and lowered her long lashes to cover her eyes.

"Ineye, you know how I feel about you,' she said quietly but desperately.

'Oh yes, I know. I know I was always second best to Richard, but I was hoping. I thought that maybe one day you'd fall out of love with Richard, forget him maybe and love me instead. But I suppose now, I'd better stop hoping,' Ineye said and laughed. It was a false, hollow laugh.

Mina could say nothing. She took a quick glance at him and saw the hurt and disappointment on his face.

She was sorry but there really was nothing she could do to help him. She had a lot when Richard was away but she had known all along that if Richard were around he would stand no chance.

'Good luck Mina,' Ineye said.

'Thank you, Ineye. I'm sorry, Mina said quietly. Ineye really was a nice boy but he had never been able to set her whole body on fire, like Richard could, just by looking at her. She had wanted no one else since she met Richard. She knew that Ineye still wanted to marry her, even though she had two children, but she did not want to marry him. Right now, she wasn't even sure what she wanted to do.

After lunch, they started packing Miatta's things together.

'Mummy, why is Miatta going home? Why can't she just stay here?'

'Oh no, I can't. Pop will be all alone. Why can't we all stay together in Pop's house instead?' Miatta countered.

Mina ignored them and went on packing. She knew that they would pursue the matter until she gave them a definite and favourable reply but she went on stalling for time.

'Yes, why?' repeated Bindo.

'Hmm, why what?' Mina feigned ignorance.

'I said why can't we all stay in daddy's house?' Bindo asked.

Miatta, has your daddy got a house of his own?' Mina asked.

No. We are staying in a guest house but Pop says he'll soon get an apartment,' Miatta informed them.

'Okay why don't we wait until he does get one?' Mina smiled.

"You mean, we'll all stay together if he does get one?' Miatta wanted to know.

"That's a matter for your daddy to decide, darling, Mina said.

Richard would not come in when he called for them as they were all ready. They all got into the car and drove off. The twins chattered happily, on their way to the park, unconcerned by the silence between their parents.

I'm going to go on the Scrambler Twist — that's the most exciting one, the Astro-wheel and the flying Jumbos. Oh, I love everything, Miatta. I'll tell you what to do. Lola told me they've got a ghost train there now,' Bindo prattled.

'You won't catch me going on that. I want to go on the round-about. Oh, I'm so excited!' Miatta cried, Bindo's excitement rubbing off on her. 'I'm so excited!' she exclaimed over and over again.

'Daddy, did you bring this car from Liberia?' Bindo asked her father.

'No, I hired it here in Lagos the day after we arrived. That's why it has this label 'C.H.S., ' Richard explained to her, pointing to the sticker.

'That means Car Hire Service.' Miatta said knowingly

'How did you know that?' Mina asked in surprise.

'Pop told me,' Miatta smiled proudly. They got to the Park and Bindo dragged her father to the Ticket Office, where they bought two booklets. The girls called to their parents and waved excitedly while they were enjoying some of the smaller rides.

Richard used the opportunity to start a conversation with Mina. 'You are looking great today, Mina,' he complimented her, better than you looked on Wednesday. I hope Miatta was not much trouble?'

'Thank you,' Mina said, without a smile. 'Richard, you behave as if Miatta's not my child.

Of course, she's no trouble and you know it. She is such a clever, well-mannered little girl that everybody loves her.

You should have Bindo for a day. Even my mummy gave you credit for Miatta's upbringing. You did a far better job with her than I did with Bindo.

'Oh no, no!' Richard protested. It isn't all my work, really. I had a lot of help with her, you know and…

'Mamee and Mrs. Wallace?'

'Yes, how did you know?' Richard was not too surprised. "Miatta? Mina nodded:

'Yes, I guess you know I work for Mr. Wallace. He owns a publishing company and I am heading the new branch just opened here in Lagos.

Mr. and Mrs. Wallace have four children. Two were already at college in America when we got to Liberia. The younger two left only three weeks ago to start college. So Miatta was sort of Mrs. Wallace's baby. It was she who got us Mamee.

Mamee's children are all grown up too so Miatta was her baby too?'

'How come she is not spoiled?' Mina was surprised. If both women had doted on the little girl, she would have had a tendency to get spoiled.

'You know me, Mina. I would never allow that, and the Wallaces, even though they are Americans they are firm with children. And anyway, I guess Miatta is just a child that will grow up naturally unspoilt.

You women tend to spoil children. I'm sure you've all smothered Bindo with love, as she is the baby in your family.'

'But Richard...' began Mina feebly.

'Don't get me wrong, Mina. I'm not criticising you, only I know you, don't I?' Richard cut in with a smile:

Mina smiled too.

The twins came running along breathlessly just then and asked for tickets to go on the Super rides. After some time, Miatta had had enough but Bindo wanted another ride on the Dodge'em cars. Miatta asked her father if they could have some ice cream.

'Yes, let's go and buy some,' Richard said. Mama, do you mind if we leave you to look after Bindo? We'll soon be back, Miatta said, turning to her mother.

Mina did not mind at all and said she would be quite content to wait there, while they went for the ice cream.

'Pop' Miatta began slowly, on their way to the ice cream counter. 'Why can't we all live together — you, mama, Bindo and me — like a real family?'

'Where would we stay?' Richard asked.

You said you were going to get an apartment soon.

We will live there. I know you don't like living at grandpa's but I know Mama will not mind living in our house,' Miatta said seriously.

'How do you know that? It's been a long time since your mama and I lived together and she might not want to live with me ever again. But look Miatta, if you want to stay with her for some time, you can, I won't mind.' Richard's voice was reassuring.

'Oh no, Pop! Miatta protested quickly. 'I don't want to leave you all alone. But I'd love to stay with both mama and you and Bindo too, because I love you all.

And mama says it's for you if you still want her.'

'Did she really?' Richard asked in surprise. 'Well, I shall have to ask her and hear what she has to say then.

Wouldn't you like to stay at their place for the moment? It looks to me as if you do, but are only thinking of me. Never mind, I shall be all right. I shall be going to work, you know, and I still have to get an apartment.

'Oh Pop, can I? Thank you!' Miatta cried, hugging her father.

Bindo had already finished her ride and was talking animatedly to her mother when they got back with the ice cream. Soon their parents decided it was time to go. While they were driving out of the park. Richard asked Mina if it was alright for Miatta to stay with them for some time.

'Oh Richard, can she?' Mina asked. She was so pleased. She was not sure she'd heard properly. Bindo too was delighted and gave a shout of joy. When they were almost near the Ereins' house, Richard asked Mina if she would like to go out with him the next day.

Mina, startled, replied, 'I don't know.'

'Perhaps you don't like going out, but I want to get you away from your usual surroundings so that we can talk,' Richard said.

'I don't mean that. I mean, what about the girls?' The protest sounded feeble even to her ears.

'Miatta and Bindo? Oh, don't give me that. They!! be alright,' Richard said sternly. 'Your parents' house is full of people to look after them.

'All right then Richard, when shall it be?'

Mina did not start getting dressed the next day, until Richard arrived. She had not been able to make up her mind whether to go or not, even though she had said she would. She remembered the parties and dinner dates she'd attended in the past, since he left her.

She had fast gained a reputation for extreme coolness. Very few people who had undergone a few hours of her quiet politeness, cared to be in her company again. Also, where he was concerned, she knew that she was very vulnerable or else why should she entertain him so, after all he'd put her through? The twins rushed in and stopped her wandering thoughts.

'Do hurry up, Mama,' Miatta urged her.

'Yes, so that you can come and tell us what happened before we go to bed,' begged Bindo.

Not likely! You'll have gone to bed before I come back,' their mother laughed.

'Come on Miatta. Let's go and tell daddy she is almost ready,' Bindo said and they rushed downstairs again.

"She'll be ready soon,' Miatta told her father and whispered something in his ear.

It's rude, Miatta, to whisper in somebody's ear when there are other people around.'

Bindo, anxious to know what Miatta had said, pulled at her sister's hand and declared that they were going to bring mummy down.

'I asked him where he was taking her, that's all,' Miatta told her on the stairs.

'And what did he say?' Bindo asked.

'You heard him. He said it is rude to whisper in people's ears when other people are around.'

'How do I look?' Mina asked them. 'Beautiful' chorused both girls, hugging and kissing her.

They went downstairs together and on the last stair, Miatta tripped and fell down. Richard was alone in the sitting-room. He rushed to pick her up at once. His eyes met Mina's over Miatta's head and held them for a minute, then Mina lowered her eyes and looked at Miatta's knee. She was embarrassed and asked if Miatta was all right.

'Yes. It was only a little fall, Mama.'

'No bruises?' asked Richard.

No bruises. Put me down, Pop, and go on,' Miatta said struggling to get down. Richard put her down and looked at Mina. 'That's a lovely dress you've got on Mina. You look beautiful, if I may say so.'

'Of course you may!' cried Miatta.

149

'Shut up, Miatta. Thank you, Richard.' Mina smiled. The twins looked at each other and started giggling.

Naughty girls!' Richard laughed indulgently.

"Pop, why not kiss her?' Miatta asked.

'Miatta!' Both Mina and Bindo exclaimed. Richard was amused,

"Why not?" he asked her and 'May I?' with a grand bow.

Mina laughed self-consciously as Richard kissed her lightly on the lips. Both girls laughed, clapped and cheered as their parents said goodbye and thankfully went out.

Chapter 8

'Where are we going?' Mina asked

'Where would you like to go?' Richard asked her.

'You know I have to get to know a lot of the new joints yet.'

'I don't know any myself,' laughed Mina. Why am I laughing like an idiot and feeling so embarrassed and nervous, she asked herself. She wondered once again if Richard could hear her heartbeats. What did he want to talk to her about? Was it a divorce or reconciliation?

Richard glanced at her and saw how nervous she was.

She was shaking visibly. Mina hasn't changed at all, he said wordlessly.

Relax Mina, I'm not going to eat you. You can feel at ease with me,' he smiled at her. That was it. Mina burst into tears so suddenly that he almost hit the car in front of them. Richard quickly pulled into a corner and stopped the car.

I am sorry for breaking down like this' Mina apologised through her tears, trying to clean her face. 'It's only that it's been too much for me, these past few days.

It was hell while you were away. But for Bindo, I don't know what I would have done.'

'I know, Mina, I am very sorry for all I put you through, but you made it so clear you were not ready to leave your parents' house. If I had stayed here any longer I would have gone mad. Believe me, Mina.'Mina burst into a fresh flow of sobs. 'But Richard, it was cruel of you, to keep silent for seven whole years.

Do you hate me that much?' she said convulsively, her tears falling unrestrainedly.

'Mina, I can only say I'm sorry for my silence all these years. I didn't know it meant anything to you...?' Richard said uncomfortably.

"You didn't know it meant anything to me? Oh Richard, how can you say that? Even if I never wanted to see you again, wouldn't I want to see my child? And did you never want to see Bindo all these years?' Mina asked him, frantic in her grief.

I've said I'm sorry. You know me and my pride. I guess that's what caused all these but Mina, we can't talk here. Let's go to the Federal Palace Hotel,' Richard said, and waited for her to compose herself before driving out of the corner where he had parked.

They drove in silence to the Federal Palace Hotel and ordered their drinks and a simple meal. They sat by the sea-side and while they were waiting for the food to arrive, with the cool night wind blowing gently at them, Richard started explaining.

'Of course I wanted to see Bindo but I knew where. you were and I knew that she was safe with you, I should have known you wouldn't have that sort of assurance, but Mina, I was really hurt by what you did to me. I was determined to put you out of my mind. I told Miatta about you but I made her promise never to ask for you. Time just slipped right away. Before I knew it, she was a big girl."

The waiter brought the food and Richard paused.

'As I told you, after we left your parents' house we went to Kano where I had friends of my own. Mr. Wallace was over on a tour from Liberia. He offered me a job in his Publishing Company. Mr. Wallace acted as a surrogate mother for Miatta and later found Mamee to act as her nurse. They taught Miatta a lot of things. At five, she could tell the time and she went to music lessons with Andy and Sandra Wallace.

'I hear they have gone to America, 'Yes, they've gone to finish their high school there. And that was partly why we came home. Sandra and Andy could not talk of anything else and Miatta became sad and withdrawn. She told me she wanted to go to Nigeria because they were going to America. Incidentally, Mr. Wallace had just opened a new branch here in Lagos and had asked me if I would like to come home and manage it. I hadn't given him a definite reply. I wasn't sure if I was ready to take on you and your family yet.'

Richard paused conscious of his tactlessness.

'Have you got any staff yet?' Mina asked, with polite interest, avoiding the dangerous topic.

"Yes. Mr. Wallace has friends here. He came over and practically everything was set before I came.' There was another pause. Then he went on, 'Mr. and Mrs. Wallace were always talking to me about making up with you. I wasn't sure if you'd grown up yet. I could not bring myself to forgive you for not coming along with me when I needed you.'

He stopped again and wondered if his words sounded as smug to her as they did in his own ears. But he had firmly believed that a wife's place was with her husband.

He still believed it. She should be willing to cut off all old ties and uproot herself if need be, to go to the ends of the world with her husband. But not Mina. She was still tied to her mother's apron strings. She had no intention, he was sure then, of leaving the comforts and luxuries of her father's house and starting with him. She had said so in almost so many words herself. It would be painful for the only daughter of the Ereins to go and set up a home, not as big as her parents' house.

I felt your place was with me but you thought it was with your parents. That did something to me, Mina, I didn't want to listen to anyone who advised me to settle with you. Anyway when I saw how much Miatta wanted to come home, it made up my mind for me. I told the Wallaces, I would come home and that I would see you.

If you had not got anyone else, I would try my best to see that things are patched up between us,' he finished.

'You are still my husband. I never forgot that, even though I didn't know where you were. So there never was anybody else,' Mina said lamely:

'Well, there was never anyone else for me too. Oh - don't get me wrong — I am still a normal male, with all the natural drives. I didn't exactly live the life of a monk. There were girls but no special one. Oh God, I'm sounding like a male chauvinist pig to you, aren't I?'

'No, you are not, you're just being truthful,' Mina smiled at him.

'Mina, I know I have no right to ask you for another chance, I mean, to let us try again. But I think for the twins' sake, we can both forget the past. If you are willing, we could start again.' He paused and waited for Mina to talk, but she continued eating, so he went on.

I don't really want you to give me a definite answer today. If you say yes, I'd be delighted. If you say no, I wouldn't blame you because I know what I've done to you. I know you must think I've got a nerve, walking out on you like that and coming back unannounced. I'm not expecting you to welcome me with open arms.

I don't mind whatever you say about me, but I'd really like you to give it a thought. I want the best for those two girls, and I'm sure you do too. That's why I had to see you and talk to you alone. On the other hand, I'll understand if you want a divorce.'

Mina pushed her plate away before taking a sip of her bitter lemon. She was not sure what she really wanted from Richard any more. Oh yes, she thought he had a cheek. Imagine him expecting her to forgive and forget what he had made her go through. Even though she wanted her children to have the best of family life, she could not bring herself to agree to living with him again, not so soon.

I shall have to think about it, Richard. Please give me time, Richard; you've hurt me too much to forget quickly,' she said brokenly. 'I'm not sure that I know what to do.'

'Of course,' Richard said. "You can think about it for as long as you want. I understand. You need to consider all the pros and cons of living with an ogre like me again.'

Mina laughed and told him how she had managed with Bindo. It was very late by the time she got home.

The girls and her mother were asleep. Only her father was still awake. going through some papers in his study. Mina sank down on a sofa in the study.

'How was your evening?' her father asked, and seeing the puzzled expression on her face, explained, 'I mean has he changed much?'

'No,' smiled Mina and she told could not bring herself to agree to living with him again,

'I shall have to think about it, Richard. Please give me time, Richard; you've hurt me too much to forget quickly,' she said brokenly. 'I'm not sure that I know what to do.'

'I don't know. I don't know what I feel for him or what he feels for me anymore. I feel he is asking us to start again just because of Miatta and Bindo...' And is that not good enough?' her father interrupted her.

'It is — in a way,' replied Mina. 'But it's our lives too. It would be sheer agony if I went to live with him, and you know, he treated me no better than a housekeeper who shared his bed. Daddy, it's been so long. I can't just forgive him for all the misery he's caused me just yet. Sometimes I feel as if I hate him for what he did.'

'I know,' nodded her father sympathetically. 'But you don't hate him, Mina. You love him and very much too'

'How do you know that?'

Mina, I am your father and I've watched you grow up from a baby into a girl and then a woman. Do you think I don't know what you went through when Richard took Miatta away? How do you think I felt when he turned up here on Wednesday night after so many years? I felt like throwing him out, strangling him, anything - but you stopped me from even reprimanding him.

The look on your face that day, Mina. I'll will never forget. You looked so radiant, so happy, as if you had come alive again. I told your mother not to interfere too or Richard would have heard from us by now. And since then, you have changed so much. Look at you!

You are filling out properly. Mina, my daughter, you love Richard better than anyone in this whole wide world that has been his saving grace with me and your mother.

This is my day for listening to long speeches. Mina mused, wondering if her father was right.

'Anyway, did you enjoy this evening?' her father's voice brought her thoughts to a halt. She nodded, wondering why he asked."So you know you are off to a good start, Mina. You know he is your friend. He likes you, even if he doesn't love you. That's a good start. With those two up there, I'm sure you can work it out between you.

Anyway, you must think about it all by yourself. Search your mind thoroughly and listen to your inner self. If you love him as much as I think you do, you will forgive him and forget in time. Remember always that marriage is not a bed of roses. You have to work hard at it, to make a go of it. If it's a rose, it will blossom,' her father advised her.

Mina thanked him. It was a long time ago since she talked to her father like this, heart to heart. She thought about the last sentence a lot before she could fall asleep at last in the early hours of the morning.

The twins woke her up far too soon.

'Mama, did you have a nice time?' Miatta asked and Mina nodded.

'What happened?' Bindo wanted to know.

'You have to go to school, you know. I'll tell you when you come back. All right?' she smiled at them.

'Oh tell us now, please mummy,' they both pleaded, but Mina would not.

'No,' she said firmly. 'After school.'

As soon as Mina came back from work, they gave her no peace until she told them about her date with their father. 'Why are you so inquisitive, both of you?' she laughed. 'Now sit down and listen carefully to me.' They both sat down and faced her.

'Your daddy has asked for us all to live together again,' she began.

'Hurrah! exclaimed Bindo gleefully.

'And what did you say?' her sister asked more quietly.

I told him I'll have to think about it. It's been such a long time since...

'Why did you say that, mama? Don't you love him anymore?' Miatta asked.

You know nothing about love, my dear. Real love is two sided. I don't think your daddy and 1 are in love any more,' Mina explained.

'But he loves you, I know he does mama, and you love him too, Miatta persisted. 'Please mama, say yes.'

'Anyway, I'm still thinking about it. But I doubt if it will work out as much as you think it will,' Mina shrugged.

A week later, Mina had still not made up her mind and the girls were still living with her even though Richard had now found a flat. Bindo did not think it was such a bad idea for them to live in her grandparents' house, as it was where she had lived all her life. But Miatta was not happy about it. She wanted to go to her father but she did not know how to tell her mother.

It was impossible to tell her father so when he telephoned, because her mother was always around. Confused and unhappy, Miatta hid her feelings for as long as she could. Then she fell sick.

Chapter 9

Doctor Candido, a middle-aged gentleman, who had been the Ereins' family doctor for years, gave Miatta a thorough checkup but could find nothing physically wrong with her. He put it down to the change of environment and prescribed some vitamins for her. Mina took her home and put her to bed.

'Mama, I want Pop. Please tell him to come.' Miatta told her mother. So Mina called Richard at his office and told him Miatta was ill and asked him. It was almost a week since Richard came last to see them. He came at once, and Miatta put her hands in his. 'Pop, don't go away any more,' she said. Richard asked Mina when the illness started and she told him what the doctor said.

Richard looked at her sitting on the edge of the bed, looking so anxious and worried. 'Don't look so worried, Mina.' he said.'Miatta is a plucky little girl. It will only be for a few days at most and then she'll be okay.'

'I can't help being worried. She couldn't sleep all night and she won't eat anything,' Mina said anxiously.

'That's probably because her mouth is bitter. But since the doctor has said it is nothing serious, you shouldn't worry.'

'I suppose so. Poor you, we've disrupted your schedule,' Mina sympathised with him, knowing he was a very busy man.

'Don't worry about me. I'll stay until she wakes up, if it's alright with you?' Richard said.

'Of course it is. Would you like anything? A drink, newspapers?

'No, don't worry I'm okay ' He smiled at her.

'But you will have some lunch, won't you, Richard?'.

'Please don't bother.'

No, it's no bother. What will you eat?' Mina persisted.

Anything you are having for lunch will be fine with me — I mean, you can't ask the cook to start preparing something else now.'

'It's not the cook. I'm cooking it myself. Anyway, I know what you'd like. Why don't you read while I cook? I've still got some of your books in that bookshelf over there', she said, pointing as she went out.

Richard, alone in the room, glanced round. He noticed that it was not very different from the way it was before he left. Now there was another chest of drawers and an Ottoman chest, probably for Bindo's things. The room was as neat as ever. Richard smiled wryly as he went to get the book. Mina was one for orderliness.

She always had been obsessed by this idea of everything being spick and span. Just as he got himself a book he had particularly liked those days, Miatta's eyelids fluttered open. 'Pop?' she whispered.

'Yes, I'm here.' Richard answered, taking hold of her hand.

'Let's go home,' she said.

Richard was amazed. Not in a million years would he have thought that she was sickening for him. 'Okay, we shall,' he said.

'Are you better now?' 'I don't know, Pop. My head aches and my tummy too 'Never mind. You'll soon be all right,' her father said soothingly.

'Pop, I want to go home with you', Miatta said, just as Mina came into the room.

'You'll go, don't worry,' Richard told her. Mina, with tears in her eyes, stood where she was. Miatta closed her eyes and drifted off in a feverish sleep again.

'She wants to go home? Is that why she's ill?' Mina enquired from Richard. He nodded and she burst into tears. 'Oh, my God!' she sobbed. 'And I thought she was happy here!'

'Don't be like that. Of course, she is happy. It's only that the change's been too sudden for her to adjust to so early. She's got too used to me to stay away for long just yet. And all her life. she's always turned to me when she is ill, Richard said.

Mina went on crying and Miatta woke up again

'Please don't cry, mama — I'm going to be all right.' She had been woken up by Mina's sobbing and excessive cuddling. She was surprised to find Mina crying and when her mother went on weeping, she became frightened and puzzled. 'I'm not going to die, am I?' she asked, alarmed, looking at her father.

Mina hastily cleaned her face. 'Oh no, my darling, "you are not.' she said, 'you are going to get well and jump about with Bindo. Don't mind me, I cry a lot, you see. You'll have to get used to that.' She smiled weakly and went out to get the food.

Between them, they made Miatta eat a little. Then she slept again after taking her medicines and Mina decided it was time to talk to Richard. She had been thinking seriously and knew what she would do. She did not want her children to be unhappy and for them, she would sacrifice her doubts about the success of their marriage.

"Richard,' she began. 'I've thought and thought about us, and it is Miatta who has helped me come to a decision. I'll do anything for my children. I think in their best interest, my answer is yes, let's start again.' Richard was surprised.

'Are you sure? I mean after...'

I'm sure,' Mina sighed, looking him straight in the eyes. 'I've put a lot of thought into it. I loved you very much once, and I went through hell when you left. I know I made a lot of mistakes before too, but you don't correct one wrong with another wrong. I am grateful to God for this second chance he's giving me, for my children to have a home with two parents.'

'Mina, I want you to be quite sure,' Richard said seriously.

'I am,' she smiled, with tears in her eyes.

'Thank you. I hope you won't regret it,' 'Richard said seriously.

The girls were thrilled when they were told. Bindo danced around the house and told everyone they were going to live in her father's house. Mina's father had no objections whatsoever. Her mother agreed that it was good news, and went up to see Miatta.

'How is she?' Mrs Erein asked her daughter.

'She's better now that she knows we are going to live with her father,' Mina smiled.

'Are you going back to him because she is ill?' 'I'm going back to him because it is what I want to do, I suppose. I still love Richard, despite everything.

I want to spend the rest of my life with him and the twins,' Mina said looking at her fingers.

'Well, I hope you know what you are doing and are sure. I wish you all the best,' her mother said.'Thank you, mummy Honestly. I do know what I'm doing. Funny, Richard himself asked me if I was sure, Mina smiled.

Richard came to take them to see his house a couple of days later, when Miatta was better. It was a three bedroom flat — a large bedroom and two smaller ones, one of which contained a bunk bed, and the other, a single divan bed. He also took them to his neighbours upstairs and introduced them.

In less than one week, they moved in. Mrs. Erein gave Mina one of her housemaids to take along as a house help. Richard had no objections so Abigail went with them. Miatta and Bindo were so excited on their first night in their father's house. They talked late into the night, both declaring they would never be able to sleep but of course they did.

Mina sat in her office thinking about her life with Richard. She wondered what she would have done without her daughters. They were everything to her and in their own childlike way, they tried all their best to bring their parents together. Today, it was six weeks since they had come back together but they still behaved for most of the time with polite restraint.

It was his birthday tomorrow and Mina wondered what she would give him. She did not know what to buy or to do. The twins were making him something, but were keeping it a secret from her.

Except for Miatta and Bindo, there seemed to be no life in their house. Richard was nearly always serious when she was there. She thought about it as she tidied her desk and wondered if she had done the right thing.

Yes, she had. She needed nothing but the obvious happiness in her daughters' lives to know she had. Miatta and Bindo worked, played and fought with each other.

The worst of their fights had been one night when they were going to have a bath before going to bed.

Miatta got to the bathroom first and started running the bath. She was taking her clothes off, while the bath was filling up, when Bindo rushed into the bathroom. She was about to jump into the bath when Miatta pulled her back. 'You met me here, Bindo,' she said.

'But I pulled my clothes off before you. I don't have to wait for you to finish taking your clothes off, before I take my bath,' Bindo countered.

'Yes, you have!' Miatta argued.

'It's your own stupid fault for being so slow, not mine,' her sister snapped.

'Don't call me stupid and slow, spoiled little Riche Rich!' Miatta said.

Bindo saw red. Richie Rich was the name the boys at school and most girls called her behind her back. She hated that name and it always brought out the worst in her. She gave Miatta a very hard slap on the cheek and Miatta screamed, because she had not expected it. She gathered all her strength and gave Bindo a harder one.

Then they started fighting, and Bindo dug her long, sharp nails into Miatta's cheek. Miatta screamed loudly again as the cut started bleeding.

Mina rushed into the bathroom followed closely by Richard. 'What happened?' she asked anxiously, separating them. Miatta took one look at her father and began to cry. He had ordered her never to fight. If anybody annoyed her, she always had to report to him or any older person around. This was the first time she had to disobey that order and she was sorry.

'Go on, say something. Why are you crying? Bindo taunted her.'But I was the one who ran the bath, not you Bindo, so why should you take your bath before me?' Miata protested.

'It's not my fault you were slow,' said Bindo, looking angrily at Miatta, 'And then she called me "spoiled" little "Richie Rich." So I slapped her.'

'But you called me stupid first of all, that's why I said so,' Miatta cried.

'Will you stop that noise, Miatta, what are you crying for? Next time you quarrel or fight with somebody of your age, and I see you crying, I'll deal with you, do you hear me?' Richard stormed, shaking her,

Mina took Miatta away from his grip and he went out.

She took both their hands and said, 'Bindo, you should have waited to take your turn. She got there before you and if she had locked the door, you wouldn't have been able to get in. Then you should watch your temper and your tongue. You shouldn't have called her stupid, and you shouldn't have slapped her. And Miatta, stop calling Bindo a spoiled rich girl. You know it's not very good of you, Bindo's no richer than you are. If they call her Richie Rich at school, you should be able to defend her and deal with them. Now, I'll leave you both.

She hugged them both after saying this and left.

Bindo went into the bath fuming with rage and talking under her breath.It's not fair. All the time, it's Bindo. Bindo! You shouldn't have done that! Bindo, stop it! They always take sides with both of them. One day, I'll just leave this house and go back to my grannie's house. I hate all of them.' She muttered angrily.

Miatta stood by patiently and watched her take her time with her bath. 'I'm sorry, Bindo,' she apologised.

"You don't have to be,' Bindo replied in a voice that sent Miatta aback.

She said nothing more until they went to bed. She said goodnight and apologised again.

'Goodnight!' Bindo answered coldly, turning her back.

Next morning, Miatta was surprised to find that Bindo was still angry with her. She chatted as they were dressing for school, but Bindo did not reply. The only thing Bindo said to her that morning was, 'That's my slip you are wearing.'

'Oh?' Miatta said apologetically. 'I thought you wore yours yesterday.

I did not. Maybe you did not look well. Anyway, they are both mine.' Bindo said coldly, stretching out her hand for the slip. Miatta pulled the slip and gave it to her. She was surprised Bindo wanted the slip back.

They had always worn each other's things and there had been no arguments about that. But if Bindo wanted her to stop wearing her things, then she would stop. She took another slip which was hers and wore it.

'Shall I help you fold your nightie?' she asked, anxious to make up.

'No, I'll do it myself!' Bindo snapped. 'All right, shall I clean your shoes?'

'No! They've already been cleaned. Just leave me alone!' Bindo shouted at her. But I've said I am sorry, Bindo, Miatta said, surprised.

'And did I say you weren't? I just want to be left alone,' Bindo told her coldly.

All through that day, Bindo did not speak to Miatta at school. She replied only in monosyllables, when Miatta spoke to her. After school, when they got home, Miatta asked Bindo if they could do their homework together.

Bindo could take no more. 'Look, Miatta, leave me alone. I hate you. I don't want to talk to you ever again!' she shouted at her sister.

Miatta was shocked at Bindo's outburst. All her defenses snapped and she could think of nothing else. 'I hate you.' The phrase kept ringing in her head like a bell.

When Mina came home, she noticed that both girls looked sad. 'What's happening here?" she asked. 'Nothing,' Miatta replied much too quickly for Mina not to guess something was wrong. Bindo said nothing and did not even look at her mother.

Some few minutes later, Mina and Abigail were busy in the kitchen when Miatta came in, looking very sad and worried.

'Mama, I'm sorry about yesterday. Please, tell Bindo to talk to me,' she said in a low voice.

Mina stopped what she was doing to look at her daughter. Miatta's lower lip was trembling

'What?" Mina asked in surprise. 'Bindo won't speak to me. I've said I'm sorry several times but she won't speak to me. She says she hates me.' Mina could see Miatta was making a great effort not to cry. She pulled her into her arms and said, cradling her, 'She doesn't hate you, darling. She's only angry.

You must know that she loves you very much.Let's go and see her.

They found Bindo lying on her bed, working on a jigsaw puzzle. She looked up as they came in and went on fixing her jigsaw pieces together.

'I want to talk to you, Bindo,? Mina said. Bindo sat up.

'What is this I hear about you not talking to Miatta?

She's sorry about yesterday and she's told you so, I hear.'

'I don't want to talk to her or any of you. I hate all of you.' Bindo said, pouting her lips.

Mina flinched. She thought for a minute and smiled to herself. "I'm sorry about that. I didn't know you felt that way about us. Hate is a very strong and ugly word.

I don't think you know what it means. I pray you never do because a child of God never hates. Let's just say you don't like us just now but we love you very much, all three of us. Remember that!' she said and left the room. Bindo burst into tears.

'Don't cry Bindo, I'm sorry, Miatta said quietly. I'm sorry too, Miatta,' Bindo said through her tears. She got up from the bed and went into the kitchen. She stood by the door and apologised. 'I'm sorry, mummy.

'That's all right.' Mina smiled at her. 'I don't hate you. It's only that whenever there's any quarrel between Miatta and me, daddy always takes sides with her and you too, mummy,' Bindo complained.

Mina came out of the kitchen and took them both in her arms.

'Now look here, both of you, just because you've not been living together - I mean, just because Miatta has been living with your daddy, doesn't mean I don't love her as much as I love you, Bindo. And just because you have been living with me all your life does not mean your daddy doesn't love you,' she told them.

'But you always take sides with Miatta. Everything she does is right,' Bindo persisted, trying hard not to burst into tears again

'Bindo,' Mina said. 'I don't love you any less because Miatta's here and I'm sure your daddy doesn't love Miatta less because of you. If you are right, I will say so and if Miatta is, I will say so too. So don't let there be any rivalry between you.

Run off now. Daddy will soon be back and the food is not ready yet.' That had been the end of that quarrel, and somehow they had understood what she told them.

It was Richard's birthday. Mina found herself thinking of the first birthday present she had given him, as She prepared the breakfast. She had been so unsure of herself, as unsure of his feelings for her then as she was now. She had felt as shy as a new bride. Even now. she was not sure of his feelings for her at all. It was as if he was merely living with her because of the twins. She knew how she felt about him. She loved him very much... she wished he could love her even half as much as he used to. She knew he tried, as much as possible, to make her feel at ease with him, but she knew there was something still missing.

Chapter 10

'Those children upstairs! Can't they ever learn to play quietly?' Mina complained yet again.

'They are only kids. They don't know any other ways to enjoy themselves,' Richard said. 'By the way, Mina, did you go up to thank Alhaja for the buns she gave us?' he added, his eyes glued to the rock group that was playing on the television.

'Yes. I thanked her when I saw her hanging out some clothes on the line,' Mina replied.

'You should have gone up to thank her, Mina. You know, if we are going to be neighbours of the Apatas for long, you should be friendly with Alhaja, ' Richard said, turning down the volume of the musical.

'We don't have anything in common,' Mina said defensively.

"How do you know you don't? You are both mothers. Anyway forget it,' her husband said.

Mina picked up a magazine and started filling the cross-word puzzle. Her mind was not in it, though. She found it difficult to relate to the Apatas. They were always going out attending parties, leaving their four children to amuse themselves at home. The children were very noisy and swore a lot, so Mina did not encourage her twins to play much with them. As for Mrs. Apata, she was friendly enough but Mina could not stand her. She had bleached her skin so much that it reminded Mina of a skinned chicken and she had three or four gold teeth.

Her husband was the landlord and they were both nice really but they were not the type of people Mina was used to. She was just learning to cope

'It's such a long time since I saw Johnny Marsh. 1 think I'll go and see him tomorrow. Would you like to come with me?' Richard broke into her thoughts.

'No — I mean the girls will be all alone at home,' Mina said quickly.

"They won't be alone. Abigail will be with them and you said to yourself how conscientious she is. Mina, you don't have to be with them all the time — you are smothering them.'

'But I'm not with them always. I go to work, remember?' Mina said triumphantly.

'Still you are smothering them. You should go out more but I understand - you don't like Johnny,' Richard said.

Mina said nothing. Johnny Marsh was the musician friend of Richard's who owned a rock group. She had never been able to stand Johnny and his group with their boisterous, good-humoured, ribald horseplay, and jokes which she never understood. She hadn't seen him for years now but she knew he still kept the group because she saw him on television now and then. She knew it was this talk about the Apatas and then rock group on TV that brought him to Richard's mind. She didn't want to see him, though.

'Do you want me to do anything for you before I go to Johnny's tomorrow? I'll be back late,' Richard's voice jolted her.

'That's okay by me,' she replied flatly. 'You should come with me, you know, Mina, I suppose coping with noisy old Ajegunle, and a vulgar musical is too much to bear.'"

Mina knew there was no bitterness in his words, yet they stung her. She turned to him sharply, tears instantly pricking at the back of her eyes. 'That's not fair, Richard. You are telling me I'm a snob.

'Well, be honest with yourself, Mina. Wasn't that one of the first things I said to you? And aren't you still?' Mina gasped in amazement and stared at him. How could he think such a thing of her?

Richard looked at her and said in a kind voice, 'Why else don't you want to go to Johnny's? What has he or any of his group ever done to you? I always told you not to mind their pranks, and you know in your heart that they are a good bunch. Then what about the Apata, kids? Be honest with yourself, Mina.'

I... because I...' began Mina but her words stumbled to a halt and Richard laughed loudly. He got up and switched the telly off.

'You'll never think of another reason, my dear wife. Never mind, there are worse things than being a snob, you know.'

Mina said nothing, so he went and took her by the shoulders, and gently tilted her face up to his. He knew she was upset.

'You are what you are, Mina,' he said gently, just as I am what 1 am. I'm not going to change, so I don't expect you to change. I've got no right to make you a lesser person than you are.'

Mina nodded, because she could not trust herself to speak. Long after Richard was asleep, she lay awake, thinking about what he had said. She knew that they had to compromise and meet somewhere if they were going to live the rest of their lives together.

She had to stop turning up her nose at some of his friends. She must have got that habit from her mother, she told herself. It had been subconsciously of course, but children cannot help copying some of their parents' habits. One way or the other, you just like the people who brought you up. It just rubbed off on you.

Looking back at her life with Richard, he had not done anything but what he thought was best. She had caused the whole lot of unhappiness in the past because she hadn't got her priorities right. The most Richard had done, to make her do what he wanted, was to ask her to come with him to his friends' places, and that time when he was going away he had asked her to follow him. It had been her fault that he had to go and live with her parents and work for them in the first place. It wouldn't have happened if she had put her foot down.

Her parents had made every decision in her single life as well as in her married life. She knew that she had not made any real effort to know Richard's friends. She knew what she had to do. The next day, she told Richard she would go with him to Johnny's house.

'No, you don't have to. I was only joking yesterday. I know the way you feel about him.' Richard said. 'You can't stand the sight of him. Why come when you'll hate every minute you are there?'

Mina insisted she wanted to go and they drove in silence to Ajegunle, where Johnny lived with his wife and baby son. Johnny's wife, Alice, opened the door to them. Mina had never met her before. She was petite and pretty, with a soft singing voice, and a quiet manner. She was not the sort of wife Mina would have pictured for a big noisy man like Johnny, and she was surprised. Johnny had gotten married during the period when Richard was away.

She had not seen him at all since she did not expect to like him any better.

On entering their sitting-room, she could scarcely hide her surprise. It was a beautifully decorated room and very neat. Johnny was sitting on an armchair, holding his baby son who was sleeping peacefully, and a novel lay on the arm of the chair. Mina was very much surprised to find him so domesticated.

'Hello Mina.' He greeted her warmly. 'Long time no see! It's nice to have you here. I only get to hear about you through Richard.'

Mina could only manage a little nod. She was thankful when Alice came and took the sleeping child from her husband's arms.

'How are the twins?' Alice asked, in her friendly way.

'They are fine, thank you.' Mina replied, with a smile.

They must be very big girls now. I hear they give you a lot of trouble.' said Alice, still holding the baby and sitting down on the arm of the chair where her husband was sitting.

'They are terrors,' laughed Richard, and it was a love-filled laughter. 'I can't wait for them to grow up and leave the house for my wife and me.'

Everyone laughed, for he obviously had not meant his words to be taken seriously. The men took themselves off to look at Johnny's new car and Alice got up to go and keep the baby in his cot and prepare a meal for them. Mina went with her. She liked Alice instinctively and they chatted as they stood in the kitchen, watching the rice boil.

'Johnny painted the whole of this flat himself last Christmas, you know. He uses the spare bedroom as his office. He fancies himself as a lyric writer - soft and sentimental songs; nothing like the general stuff they bawl out in the group. I don't mind him shutting himself you see.' She smiled and Mina smiled too.

Do you play anything?' she asked her.

Oh no. I don't know a thing about music. When I first met Johnny, I thought he was mad. But as I got to know him, I realised he was all sorts of people rolled into one and they were all nice. I guess up on the stage; he's the complete extrovert. But the real Johnny — the home loving Johnny — can be full of fun with me and our baby. I wouldn't swap him for all the world,' Alice told her and Mina smiled again.

The men were called in to eat and after staying for about one more hour, Richard and Mina got up to go.

'Well, Mina, maybe we'll see you again some time?' asked Johnny. He asked the question in a way that indicated he did not expect to see her again for a very long time. Richard looked away and Mina said quickly. 'I hope so. Why don't you and Alice come with the baby to our house next Sunday or Saturday? Our girls love babies and they will be delighted to see him. And Miatta loves music. She'll be most happy to talk to you, Johnny? Then she added swiftly, 'That's if you haven't got anything else to do, of course.'

They both said they would be delighted to come on Sunday afternoon. Her husband's surprise showed clearly on his face, and it was clear he was delighted.

I always thought you disliked Johnny a lot,' he remarked on the way home.

"Never mind what you thought.' Mina smiled. They drove home in a companionable, contended silence.

When they got home, Richard said, 'I still can't get over you inviting Johnny and Alice.' 'And the baby.

The next day, Mina and Richard went to a party at the house of one of his new friends. Mina looked lovely in her long blue dress and once or twice, while dancing with other people, she caught Richard looking admiringly at her. She knew she looked her best, but that look in his eyes disturbed her all the same. She wished she knew how he felt about her, but she could not very well ask him.'

Mina was conscious of Richard's eyes on her body as she changed into her nightie. He was always watching her curiously these days, as if trying to find out some-thing. She had been so touchy the past six weeks that he did not cease asking her what was wrong. Now she was down in the morning and very tired too, but she would not go to the doctor's, neither would she confide in Richard. Her parents had celebrated their 45th wedding anniversary two days before and after all the running around, she became ill but she would ask if she had done as he suggested before going to work that morning.

She decided not to say anything until he brought the subject up himself. He did as soon as she got into bed and switched off the light.

"What did the doctor say?' he asked her.

"Nothing,' she replied simply.

"What do you mean nothing?' Richard frowned.

"How could he say nothing?'

'Because I did not go to see him.?

Richard was furious. He switched on the light instantly and faced her, eyes blazing. He could not understand why she would not go to see the doctor, if she was really ill. Women were so difficult to understand. She knew what to do. And he was sure if she started looking ill, thin and miserable, that mother of hers would start talking. She had been so good ever since he and Mina had settled. She minded her business and only paid them a visit once in a while, which was just as well for everybody. But he knew if Mina started looking sick or unhappy, that would stir up controversy again.

'I'm not really ill. It is only fever, I think,' he heard Mina's voice beside him.

"So what are you doing about it?' he asked her and was surprised by her reply.

'Oh don't query me! I know what to do,' she snapped angrily at him.

'Well, please yourself. Sorry I asked!' Richard said, shrugging his shoulders. He put off the light and turned his back on her.

Mina could not help feeling bad at the way she snapped at him. Here was somebody who was genuinely concerned about her welfare and she had to go and shout at him. But she was not going to apologise. She was fed up with apologising for her beastliness. What was the point of apologising if she was going to do the same thing again? She turned her own back on him too and went to sleep.

A couple of days later, she was vomiting. She had forgotten to close the bathroom door, and she did not know Richard was there, watching her. She turned around to leave the room after washing her mouth and face thoroughly and found Richard in the doorway. She wondered how long he had been there, but his next words told her she could not hide what was happening to her no longer.

You are pregnant, Mina, he stated rather than asked, looking steadily at her.

Mina did not know what to say or where to hide her face. She felt like asking the ground to open up and swallow her. She nodded slowly,

'Then why didn't you tell me? Or don't I have a right to know?' Richard continued.

I didn't know how you would take it. We've only been back together for three months and I've been pregnant for ten weeks out of the three months. I don't know what you feel about me. To come and burden you with another baby - well, I felt it would be too much for you.' Mina said, gazing at her toes..

'So what were you going to do?" Richard asked quietly, walking her to the bedroom.

'I don't know. I was just playing for time. Everyday I say to myself, 'You must tell him today, but when I see you my nerves fail me.'

Richard smiled and took both her hands in his. He looked at her straight in the eyes and said: 'I'm delighted about this pregnancy. You should know by now that I don't hold anything against you. I love you, Mina.' Mina could not believe her ears. She drew her gaze away from him and said, I thought you didn't love me any more, that you were only living with me because of the twins and nothing more. I got pregnant by mistake again this time. Oh Richard, you can't begin to imagine what I've been through.'

Her body was shaking with sobs as she talked, and she burst into tears as soon as she finished. Richard said nothing. He knew Mina needed to open up and talk. I never stopped loving you, Richard,' she went on in a wet whisper. 'And I know it was mostly my fault all that trouble that happened between us. I let my mother influence me but then i hadn't grown up.

I grew up in the years you were away. I was so worried about you and the baby, especially the baby. I tortured myself thinking about what was happening to her, what she looked like and what she thought of me, a mother who never visited nor wrote or sent things to her. I convinced myself she would grow up hating me.

'Richard, I'm very glad you told her about me. You don't know how grateful I am to you for this. I know you think I haven't grown up yet, but Richard, I have. I grew up in a hard way and I'm grateful to you for this second chance you are giving me.'

Mina dried her tears and looked expectantly at Richard. He met her eyes and nodded, not trusting himself to speak yet. Mina's long speech had floored him.

He held up his hand as if to ask her to wait.

'I knew exactly how you felt,' he began at last, his voice husky with emotion. 'I used to think of Bindo so much. If anything had happened to her while I was away, with her thinking I didn't care, I would not have forgiven myself. It must have been worse for you, just knowing you had a daughter somewhere in the world, but not knowing where.'

Bindo felt rejected. She thought you did not care for her. On a few occasions, she actually said so. I felt terrible. I managed to explain the situation to her but she was not convinced. Even now, I doubt if she believes you love her as much as you love Miatta.' Mina said through her tears.

'It must have been worse for you both,' he repeated.

'At least I knew your address. I could have written to you. I thought a clean break was best. Now, I can see it was too long, too complete.'

Richard was lost in thought. He remembered all that had happened in the past from the time he met Mina through their marriage, the party and how he broke contact with her. He would have lost any right to Bindo's love, had Mina met and married someone else or if he had done so. Miatta would not have met Mina or been loved by her. He knew they had both missed the growing years of one child each. He also knew the twins had been hard done by — all because of him. He blamed himself for all this and quite suddenly, it dawned on him what he had done to all of them, especially Mina.

'Oh my God, what a mess I made of everybody's lives.'

'Don't blame yourself, Richard?

'I know I haven't been much of a father to Bindo and I haven't been much of a husband to you, Mina. By God's grace, I'll make it up to you. I just hope it's not too late.'

'We've got this second chance,' Mina soothed.

'What's past is past. It was fate. Whatever will be, will be — that's my view.'

Richard shook his head and glanced at her. He could believe it was fate but did he have to be fate's instru-ment? he asked himself. He knew it all started from his foolish pride and unforgiving nature, plus his stubbor-ness and fierce temper. Mrs. Erein had goaded him admittedly, but if he had been a coo! headed person, he would not have gone that far.

'What's past is past,' Mina said again, as if she could read his thoughts.

'And we have a second chance,' he repeated her words. His only consolation now, was that things were better between Mina and him. He would make it up to her and the twins, he vowed silently, and took her in his arms.